the perfect wedding
DETAILS

More Than 100 Ideas for Personalizing Your Wedding

Maria McBride-Mellinger

Photographs by

Alan Richardson

HarperResource

An Imprint of HarperCollins*Publishers*

To Brett, Ryan and Evan,
who taught me it takes a family
to make a book.

THE PERFECT WEDDING DETAILS

Photographs © 2004 by Alan Richardson.

HarperCollins books may be purchased for
educational, business, or sales promotional use.
For information, please write: Special Markets
Department, HarperCollins Publishers, Inc.,
10 East 53rd Street, New York, NY 10022.

FIRST EDITION

Designed by Susi Oberhelman

Library of Congress Cataloging-in-Publication Data
has been applied for.

ISBN 0-06-052183-X

04 05 06 07 08 IM 10 9 8 7 6 5 4 3 2 1

contents

introduction

Welcome to the passionate path of wedding planning, which more than ever is an individual expression of affection and style. Every day I'm asked for advice on the best way to personalize celebrations. I wrote this book to share new ideas, focusing on the details any couple can easily create for their own wedding. Although I highly recommend that couples work with professionals to produce their weddings, since it really is the best way to feel more like a guest at your own wedding. I also know that most couples want a tangible connection to this important day. My best advice is to decide what you can realistically execute and allow plenty of time; wise planners always test-drive ideas. For example, if you're making a bouquet for the first time, make time to experiment at least once well before the wedding. Delegate projects that need last-minute fixes. Look to my previous books, *The Perfect Wedding* and *The Perfect Wedding Reception,* for complete planning advice and more resources, but be inspired by this book to design the memorable details that will imbue your day with a loving, unforgettable spirit.

ceremonial & reception flourishes

Beach or ballroom, country inn or city townhouse, the location of your wedding will determine many of the details of the day, so carefully consider your options before booking a site or investing in décor. My best advice is to work with your location: The most successful celebrations enhance, rather than attempt to disguise, their site's features. Look for "good bones"—basic structural elements that will facilitate the event. Walk through the space and note whatever first catches your eye. These are focal points to be highlighted in some way with decorative details, be it as simple as clusters of votive candles on windowsills or as bold as one lush floral chandelier hung from the center of the room. For couples who need to economize, I recommend booking the prettiest location you can afford. In my experience, the more lovely the venue, the less makeup it needs, which ultimately saves on the cost of decorating.

beach aisle runner

Sandy shores are delightful places to wed, if challenging sites to decorate. Temperamental winds, shifting surfaces, and the chance of showers all suggest a short ceremony and a simple approach. Easy to create, a pathway instantly designates a spot for guests to congregate. It's a helpful landmark in a sea of sand.

2 x 20-foot straw runner, available at shops specializing in Oriental imports

Bushel large shells

1. Put the runner in place one hour before the wedding. Unfurl it in the direction that guests will access the beach. (For long distances, use more than one runner.)
2. Stand at the spot in the sand where you plan to exchange vows. Anchor the runner in place with a pair of large shells.
3. Position shells about a foot apart along both sides of the runner.
4. Bury both ends of the runner under an inch of sand.

Variations: A path of petals, a painted or stenciled length of canvas, a row of torches, large acrylic urns of sea grass, or terra-cotta pots of daisies all make smart aisle runners.

paper & lace tables

Cozy and heartwarming, celebrations in the country absolutely pulse with familial affection—just picture the sun-dappled wraparound porch of a freshly painted farmhouse. These are places where tradition is cherished and grandma's handiwork treasured. For an all-white garden wedding with a down-home clapboard backdrop, I set kitchen tables with quilted cottons, delicate lace overlays, smooth stones, and exuberant bouquets of wildflowers.

48-inch-round folding tables, available to rent from party suppliers

Mix of garden chairs

108-inch-round quilted white cotton tablecloths, one per table, available to rent from linen services

64-inch-round lace overlays, available to rent from linen services

48-inch-wide roll of white butcher paper, available from paper suppliers

White linen napkins

2-inch-round white stones, one per dinner guest, available from garden supply centers

All-white, textured-rim dinnerware

White ceramic pitchers, one per table

Bunch of mixed field flowers per table

Clear glass tumblers instead of stemware

Glass milk bottles

Bag of quarter-pound fishing weights

Needle and white thread

Scissors

1. Determine the best place to situate the tables. Guest tables should be clustered together on a level grassy or paved-stone surface. Choose a location that is close, but not too close, to facilities. And given the choice, opt for an open or partially shaded area. Set tables about four feet apart; this will allow for chairs.

2. The cotton underskirts should reach the ground. To counter blustery breezes, sew six fishing weights, spaced equally, to the hem of each tablecloth. Top with a lace overlay and finish with two overlapping squares of butcher paper.

3. Fold napkins to rest on plates. Anchor in place with smooth stones.

4. Fill pitchers with water. Add field flowers to create centerpieces.

5. Use glass milk bottles as carafes.

Variations: Add color and charm with a change of linens—toile prints, chintzes, stripes and ginghams, point d'esprit voiles, even vintage kitchen cloths make any location feel more countrified.

ribbon curtain

Excite the senses of your guests from the moment they enter your celebration. A passageway hung with a satin fringe beckons a playful welcome with its beguiling dance. I love how the gentle caress of the satin tendrils enhances the already sensual experience of that first step over the threshold. Consider reinterpreting this idea wherever the opportunity presents itself: Create a corridor beneath a bare trellis, or frame the spot where you'll marry with a simple metal scaffold in either a semicircular or square shape, then adorn with ribbons.

2-inch wood dowel or PVC pipe, cut 4 inches longer than the width of the entryway

1 pair J-hook brackets to support dowel/pipe

Yards of ribbon

Tape measure

Scissors

Plastic sleeving

1. Install brackets to support the bar above the entryway. Simple J-hook brackets work best. If creating a structure and/or hanging it from the ceiling, allot enough space to allow clearance for all heights. Seven feet from the ground should be sufficient. If possible, situate the bar at an architecturally significant point. And note: The higher the bar or structure is set, the more dramatic the impact.

2. Measure the height of the entryway, then add one foot to the measurement to calculate the length of the ribbons. The overage will create a slight puddling effect on the floor. Cut ribbon lengths.

3. Use a basic square knot to tie ribbons to the bar. Secure ribbons one right next to another, to conceal the bar's unfinished surface.

4. The ribboned bar can be made weeks before the celebration. Roll up and sleeve with plastic when complete.

Variations: Paint the bar and allow it to peek through the ribbon knots. Or, instead of ribbons, use monofilament plastic thread to create strands of silk flowers to hang. Glue a crystal to the end of each strand to weight it properly.

tree table

The idea to create a table that wrapped around a tree trunk occurred to me when I saw a gardener's sketch of a bench that had been woven from ash branches to encircle a grand oak. I imagined a garden reception at which all the trees were transformed into shaded tables, bars, and food stations. To realize my vision, I used a round of plywood—many hardware stores will cut to order—stained mahogany to match the bark, then trimmed with a playful fringe.

60-inch-round of 1-inch-thick plywood, cut in half

4 22-inch lengths of 1 x 2-inch wood strips, for a 16-inch-round trunk

8 2½-inch wood screws

4 old wooden table legs

4 6-inch metal brackets

120-inch length of 3-inch-wide fringe

24 upholstery buttons

Hammer

Jigsaw

Sander or sandpaper

Small can mahogany wood stain

Tape measure

Thumbtack

Twine

Pencil

Level

1. Measure the perimeter of the tree trunk at a standard table height of 30 inches or a bar height of 40 inches. Ideally, the tree would be rooted on flat terrain and have a perfectly round trunk perimeter of at least 12 inches and branches high enough to allow ample headroom. Logically, the tree should also be situated within the parameters of your seating plan.

2. You'll need to cut a semicircle from the center of each plywood half to accommodate the tree trunk. For example, if the trunk is 16 inches around, you'll need to trace an arc half that size at the center of each plywood piece. To do this, make a simple protractor using a length of twine that measures half the diameter of the trunk: Use a thumbtack to anchor one end of the twine to the center point on the straight edge of each plywood half, tie a pencil to the other end, and draw the arc. Saw along the mark.

3. Sand the edges of the circle. Stain the wood. Let dry.

4. To create the brace, use wood screws to attach the wood strips along the straight edges. The one-inch side of each strip should rest perpendicular to the semicircle and be flush with the straight edge of the plywood half. Use four screws per strip, equally spaced.

5. Use wood screws to attach two kitchen legs, equally spaced, to the underside of each plywood half.

6. Prop up the plywood halves to encircle the tree. Use a level to position properly. Use a pair of wood screws to join the halves where the wood strips meet. Provide additional support from beneath by screwing metal brackets, equally spaced, directly into the tree trunk.

7. Once the table is stable, attach fringe along the edge. Hammer in place with upholstery buttons spaced five inches apart.

carpet of petals

At first sight, I knew this trellised vineyard at the edge of a pond would provide a perfectly lyrical place for a late summer celebration. The sheltered open-air space had the charming appeal of a secret garden, and the setting became that much more seductive when I showered an Oriental carpet with gladiola and dahlia petals. Well-worn patterned rugs work best, their age lending an air of Old World romance to the scene. If the carpet's edges are frayed and some sections a bit threadbare, a little dirt won't make it any worse for wear.

6 bunches or more of assorted flowers

8 x 10-foot Oriental-style carpet, to frame a 6-foot long dining table, rugs available at flea markets and carpet remnant suppliers

8 x 10-foot 2-ply plastic drop cloth

1. Remove the petals from the stems and set aside. This may be done a day or two in advance, as long as the petals are kept cool. And this is a good use of full-blown flowers that have begun to drop petals: Blooms at this stage of maturity, by the way, are frequently available at economical prices.

2. Scout locations for the rug. A level, shaded spot is ideal. For the least wear and tear on the lawn, aim for a time when conditions are dry, and plan to remove the carpet as soon as possible after the event. Use at least one rug, under the bridal table, and consider placing carpets beneath all of the guest tables. They should act as frames, with a two-foot perimeter of carpet fabric extending beyond the borders of each table. For cocktail parties indoors or out, create lounge areas by clustering upholstered seating on throw rugs.

3. Unfold the plastic drop cloth and position it exactly where you'll place the carpet. Situated underneath, it will protect the rug from moisture. Match up one end of the carpet with that of the drop cloth and unroll.

4. Once the furniture is in place and the tables are set, and just before guests arrive, scatter petals across the carpet for a lavish presentation.

Variations: Long Oriental-style hallway rugs make wonderful aisle runners. Line them up end to end as needed and blur their edges with plenty of petals.

birch wreath

Wreaths make the most romantic wedding décor. My favorites are crafted from seasonal produce and foliage. Doors and mantels are the expected backdrops for these organic sculptures, but when I encountered a bright dining room with wide glass picture windows, I knew a dramatic row of square birch wreaths would serve as the perfect accent. The silver-barked frames dressed up the room and drew attention to the picturesque snowy panorama outside.

4 30-inch lengths of 2-inch-wide birch branches

4 twiggy tertiary birch branches

4 3⅝-inch wood screws

6 30-inch lengths wired leather laces

1 bunch flowering leptosporum

1 large hydrangea head

5 stems spray roses, four flowers per stem

4 stems variegated ivy

Drill

Spool nylon monofilament, tested to support 75 pounds

Clippers

1. Up to two weeks in advance, construct the mainframe of the wreath. Five inches from each end of the wide birch branches, drill a hole almost big enough to accommodate a wood screw. Then use the screw to join two branches at a 90-degree angle. Attach additional branches to create a square.

2. Wire a tertiary branch to each juncture, twisting one length of leather lace around and around the branches to also conceal the screw.

3. Make the wintery branches seem to bloom. All around the wreath, tuck sprigs of leptosporum between the tertiary branches and the frame.

4. Up to two days before the event, create a simple bouquet of blooms. I arranged stems of spray roses and sprigs of ivy beneath a large hydrangea head. Fasten the bouquet at its base with one length of wired leather lace, then set aside in a cool room, with the stems immersed in water.

5. Plan to hang the wreath diagonally, and secure it to the window frame using nylon filament. Just before the reception, nest the bouquet in the bottom corner of the wreath, anchoring it in place with the remaining wired leather lace.

Variations: For holiday celebrations, use spray paint or metal leafing to gild branches, then attach a bouquet of antique glass ornaments. Or crisscross the frame with more tertiary branches and thread these twigs with feathers, beads, and crystals to create a contemporary dream-catcher, a Native American amulet believed to ensnare malevolent spirits and ensure emotional security—an appropriate insignia for wedding days!

carpet of petals

At first sight, I knew this trellised vineyard at the edge of a pond would provide a perfectly lyrical place for a late summer celebration. The sheltered open-air space had the charming appeal of a secret garden, and the setting became that much more seductive when I showered an Oriental carpet with gladiola and dahlia petals. Well-worn patterned rugs work best, their age lending an air of Old World romance to the scene. If the carpet's edges are frayed and some sections a bit threadbare, a little dirt won't make it any worse for wear.

6 bunches or more of assorted flowers

8 x 10-foot Oriental-style carpet, to frame a 6-foot long dining table, rugs available at flea markets and carpet remnant suppliers

8 x 10-foot 2-ply plastic drop cloth

1. Remove the petals from the stems and set aside. This may be done a day or two in advance, as long as the petals are kept cool. And this is a good use of full-blown flowers that have begun to drop petals: Blooms at this stage of maturity, by the way, are frequently available at economical prices.

2. Scout locations for the rug. A level, shaded spot is ideal. For the least wear and tear on the lawn, aim for a time when conditions are dry, and plan to remove the carpet as soon as possible after the event. Use at least one rug, under the bridal table, and consider placing carpets beneath all of the guest tables. They should act as frames, with a two-foot perimeter of carpet fabric extending beyond the borders of each table. For cocktail parties indoors or out, create lounge areas by clustering upholstered seating on throw rugs.

3. Unfold the plastic drop cloth and position it exactly where you'll place the carpet. Situated underneath, it will protect the rug from moisture. Match up one end of the carpet with that of the drop cloth and unroll.

4. Once the furniture is in place and the tables are set, and just before guests arrive, scatter petals across the carpet for a lavish presentation.

Variations: Long Oriental-style hallway rugs make wonderful aisle runners. Line them up end to end as needed and blur their edges with plenty of petals.

children's table

I am the oldest of 11 children, and in our family every celebration always included the youngest ones. Based on my own experience, I believe that kids who feel included and entertained are more likely to be happy guests. When I found out that kraft paper comes in widths to fit folding tables, I knew I'd discovered a juvenile delight. Individual bundles of crayons instantly welcome children—and encourage them to stay in their seats! Use rubber stamps in brightly colored inks to decorate the paper and label each child's place. Dress the table with pint-sized centerpieces, and drop a lollipop or other sweet treat into easy-to-handle juice glasses. Relieved parents will thank you for your thoughtfulness.

5-foot-long folding table, available for rent from party suppliers

72 x 120-inch white cotton tablecloth, available for rent from party suppliers or linen services

36-inch-wide roll of white kraft paper, calculate a 7-foot length per 6-foot table

Scissors

Double-stick tape

Assorted rubber stamps and colored inks

Alphabet stamps

6 crayons per child, assorted colors

8-inch ribbon per place setting

Short vases

Gerber daisies

1. Set up the table and cover with a basic white cotton tablecloth.
2. Cut the kraft paper so that there's a six-inch overhang at each end of the table. To create a simple hem, fold both of these flaps under to make three-inch drop-offs, then secure with double-stick tape. Along the length of the table, crease the paper with your hands to give it a customized fit. If needed, insert pieces of tape between the paper and the cloth to anchor the paper in place.
3. Decorate the paper with rubber stamps. Alphabet stamps make it easy to individualize place settings.
4. Set the table with colorful napkins ribbon-tied with bundles of crayons.
5. Use short, squat vases, minimal amounts of water, and simple, colorful flowers like gerber daisies for centerpieces.

Variations: Kraft paper is also available in a natural pigment that's well-suited for fall weddings. Have someone with a loopy script individualize the paper with colorful markers. Set tables with little amusements, like stickers, Legos, or spill-proof bottles of bubbles.

columned chuppah

Traditional Jewish ceremonies are performed under a chuppah, a covering that connotes shelter and omnipotent protection. This metaphoric structure is typically a fabric or floral canopy supported by four poles. For a formal ballroom wedding, I chose fluted columns to represent pillars of faith and community, draped them with gold-starred organza, and then topped the columns and swagged curtains with exuberant floral arrangements.

8½ yards of 108-inch-wide white organza

2 yards gold organza

6-inch star template

Can fabric adhesive spray, like 66 Glue

Can No-Fray fabric spray

2 4-inch-round Oasis domes

2 10 x 3 x 3-inch Oasis bricks

1 10-inch-wide, 3-inch-deep glass saucer

Roll ¼-inch florist duct tape

Spool heavy-duty florist wire

Florist knife

Florist clay

Scissors

6 bunches smilax vine

4 bunches roses

4 bunches dendrobium orchids

2 bunches peonies

2 bunches stargazer lilies

2 bunches calla lilies

2 baskets garden ivy

4 1 x 3-inch, 6-foot-long wood beams

4 3-inch corner metal brackets

16 1-inch wood screws

4 8-foot columns

Drill

1. Cut star shapes from the gold organza, spray with No-Fray, and let dry. Use adhesive spray to attach stars in an allover pattern to the white organza. Cut a clean edge at each end of the fabric and spray with No-Fray. This step can be done weeks in advance.

2. Submerge the Oasis bricks in water until saturated, about 20 minutes. Situate one brick in the center of the glass saucer. Trim with a florist knife to fit, or, alternately, use a portion of the second brick to completely fill the saucer. Secure brick to saucer with a crisscross of four strips of florist duct tape. Trim stems to varying lengths and insert into the Oasis to create a cascading dome of flowers. The arrangement can be prepared a day in advance as long as it is kept cool until setup.

3. Lace two 20-inch lengths of florist wire through the cage at the back of each Oasis dome. Submerge domes in water until saturated, about 20 minutes. Insert flowers and ivy stems, alternating the lengths to create a lush, elongated mix. Place arrangements on plastic sheeting in a flat cardboard box to transport to the site. Keep cool.

4. On site, arrange the columns into a six-foot square. Using the corner brackets, screw the four wood beams into a six-foot-square frame. Position the wood frame on top of the columns and anchor with a wad of florist clay in each corner.

5. Drape the organza up and over the wood frame and swag the fabric to the front left and back right columns. Tie back with the Oasis arrangements. Twist the laced florist wire lengths around the columns to secure. Style vines of smilax and select flowers so that they conceal the wire and cascade toward the floor.

6. Place the flower-filled saucer atop the front right column. Anchor in place with a large wad of florist clay.

entryway arbor

Perhaps it's because they represent the passage of time and the determination of nature, but old stone walls overrun with vines strike a poignant note. Maximize the impact of stony facades by fashioning a portal from branches of blossoming fruitwoods. I designed a fanciful arch that marries Mother Nature's bounty with mankind's ability to craft elegant objects from her elements.

Pair of carved, lightly stained wood chairs, available at flea markets

Pair of seat covers upholstered in a fabric that complements the color palette; have sewn by your local tailor or upholsterer

1 pint pickling paint

½ pint pink paint

½ pint water

2 bales flowering branches like fruitwoods or roses; keep in water until ready to use

1 bunch vibernum

1 bunch camellias

1 bunch garden roses

2 5-inch Oasis domes

Hacksaw

Superfine-grade sandpaper

Plastic tub

2 cotton rags

Clippers

Spool florist wire

Small, handheld garden spade

Hammer

8 masonry nails

8 Velcro buttons

1. Saw off the chair backs from the chair bases and discard. Use sandpaper to smooth edges and remove traces of varnish from the bases.
2. Clean the sanded, unvarnished wood and use a clean cotton rag to rub with pickling paint. Let dry, then repeat.
3. In the plastic tub, mix the pink paint with the water, then use a clean cotton rag to smudge the color over the pickled chair bases. Let dry.
4. The morning of the event, immerse the Oasis domes in water until saturated. Trim stems, then insert flowers into the domes to create a pair of lush, low arrangements. Set aside any loose petals and leftover flower heads, to be scattered later, at the site.
5. Sort through the bales of branches and select the largest ones to become the new, organic chair backs. Divide this selection in half, one for each chair. Set aside the thinner, tertiary branches, which will ultimately be used as "climbers."
6. On either side of the entryway, use a small garden spade to dig four-inch-deep holes in which to plant the large branches. Place branches no farther apart than the width of the original chair backs, so that they will appear to be "growing" out of the chair bases. Refill the holes to anchor the branches.
7. Use two-inch lengths of florist wire to attach the tertiary branches to those planted in the dirt. Taper the arrangement so that the branches narrow to a natural point as they arc across the lintel. Tap in a few masonry nails to secure the wired branches.
8. Situate the chair bases in front of the branches. Secure the cushions to the seats with Velcro buttons, one in each corner. Place one arrangement on each cushion. Scatter petals and flower heads around the chair feet.

ornament valance

Picture windows provide scenic views and brighten rooms with sunlight, but the seasonal change to winter may diminish many vistas. To make a barren landscape less obvious while still allowing precious light to fill the room, I suggest hanging a curtain of ornaments. Dangling from satin ribbons, this batch of frosted leaves perfectly captures the delicate, melancholic mood of the transition from fall to winter and camouflages the less-than-vivid environment beyond.

25 acrylic ornaments per 3-foot width of window

75 feet of ¼-inch-wide satin ribbon

Scissors

Tape measure

Curtain rod

1. Cut satin ribbon into 2½-foot lengths. Tie one end to each ornament using a basic slipknot.
2. Calculate the width and height of the window opening. Allow about one ornament for every three inches across.
3. Tie the ribbon end of each ornament to the curtain rod. Vary the lengths artfully, and stagger each strand so that the ornaments subtly "scrim" the window.

Variations: Ornament screens of all colors and shapes can be used to make a space feel more intimate, so hang them anywhere to create room dividers. There's something undeniably magical about passing through a curtain of glittering beads or tiny, tinkling bells. Simply cut the ribbons to a longer length to create the look you desire.

floral chandelier

I was married at home. My mother cultivated a vibrant flower garden that opened up onto a brick patio and a small pond, and it was indeed a charming place to say "I do." If you're planning to wed at home, or in any location that lacks a clearly defined focal point to hold the ceremony, you'll need to create such a space. One eye-catching option is to hang a floral chandelier from the limb of a tall shade tree.

Wrought-iron candle chandelier, available at garden supply centers

4 10 x 3 x 3-inch Oasis bricks, available at floral supply centers

30 stems garden roses

30 stems poppies

30 stems camellias

20 stems lilac

1 variegated ivy plant

Spool green florist tape

Wire cutters

Florist knife

Candles, one for each branch of the chandelier

Glass hurricanes, one for each branch of the chandelier

10-foot strand of chandelier crystals

1. Trim the stems and place the flowers in water for 24 hours prior to creating the arrangements, so that the blossoms will be well hydrated. The chandelier can be styled a day before the wedding, as long as the Oasis bricks are also kept well hydrated.

2. Use the florist knife to cut the Oasis bricks into three equal slices, each measuring about three inches square, for a total of 12 slices. Then, in order to fit the foam over the chandelier's candle wells, carve a hole through the center of each slice.

3. Soak the Oasis slices in water for about 20 minutes, or until thoroughly saturated.

4. Place the chandelier on a worktable. Slide one of the Oasis slices around a candle well. Use florist tape to anchor it in place. Repeat until an Oasis slice is secured to each well of the chandelier.

5. Divide the flowers and the ivy equally to decorate each Oasis slice. Use a florist knife or sharp clippers to trim flower stems to about three or four inches.

6. Insert flowers around each candle well. Full, dense flowers like camellias or lilacs cover more surface area and really make the chandelier look as if it's abloom.

7. Insert candles into the wells. Keep glass hurricanes handy to place over the candles once lit. A candle-free chandelier is also appealing for daytime celebrations.

8. Hang the chandelier in place. Once secure, drape strands of chandelier crystals between the fixture's branches. Use wire cutters to customize the lengths of the strands.

bouquets & attendant accessories

Wedding trends may come and go, but brides will always carry bouquets. The tradition of flowers at weddings dates back to the earliest times, when jubilant family and friends gathered the fruits of their community to celebrate the union. I strive to personalize tradition in every wedding I style, so that each component—from flower girl baskets to boutonnieres—reflects the couple's taste and the season in which their ceremony will take place, as well as more practical concerns. For example, when designing a bouquet, I always make sure that it won't be too cumbersome: If it is, the bride will be overwhelmed and distracted by it. Each season introduces a dozen floral options for your consideration, and each type of bloom is a contender for your affection. I suggest couples seek out seasonal flowers—they'll provide the best value. Before making your decision, be sure to explore flower markets and farmers' gardens for inspiration.

summer shell bouquet

Basic organic shapes often make the most original decorations, and I always like to incorporate the elements of the season into the ceremony. Nothing quite captures the whimsical spirit of an oceanside summer wedding like seashells, which exist in a wonderful variety of colors and forms. For a one-of-a-kind bridal bouquet, tuck them between the bluish petals of hydrangea and grape hyacinth. It's a charming way to carry the essence of the sea with you all day.

12 seashells, the best being 2-inch-long nautilus varieties, available at nautical gift shops

12 12-inch lengths of 22-gauge green florist wire

2 heads blue-and-green hydrangea

1 head blue hydrangea

20 stems grape hyacinth

Handful of beach grass

Glue gun

Spool green florist tape

Clippers

Scissors

2 yards blue organza ribbon

3 1-inch pearl-headed pins

1. Squirt a dime-sized dollop of hot glue on the inside of a shell, near its base. Immerse a half-inch of one end of a wire length in the glue and hold until fixed in place. Repeat for all the seashells, and let dry completely. The shells can be wired well in advance; the bouquet itself should be made no more than a day before the ceremony.

2. Gather together the three hydrangea. While holding them in one hand, insert the wired stems of the seashells into the bouquet. Position the shells randomly, clustering a few here and there for balance. Keep hold of all the stems to maintain the arrangement.

3. Add groups of four or five grape hyacinth stems to the outer edge of the bouquet, and gently pull some forward to give it a more relaxed, natural pattern. Review and readjust the arrangement to your satisfaction, then add the beach grass to the back of the bouquet as the final element.

4. Wrap the stems with florist tape. Begin about two inches below the flower heads and pull the tape taut as you wrap. A four-inch band of tape should be sufficient.

5. Clip stems to uniform length—about eight inches is ideal. Submerge stems in water until the wedding.

6. Shortly before the ceremony, remove the bouquet from water and pat stems dry. Cut the organza ribbon in half. Wrap one half of the ribbon over the florist tape, beginning at the top of the bouquet and spiraling down the stems. When an inch of ribbon remains, fold it under itself and anchor in place with a row of pearl-headed pins. Use the other ribbon half to tie a diaphanous bow around the stems.

spring green bouquet

One of the things I love most about spring is the vibrant reminder that, in nature, the color green is incredibly diverse. Tender foliage determined to flourish erupts in so many, many shades of green. Mint, celery, evergreen, grass—to name just a few hues—are all considered excellent accent colors. But I equally enjoy using green as the dominant shade, in combinations with itself. A verdant bouquet perfectly articulates all that is newborn and life-affirming about the season.

45 stems celadon green chrysanthemums

6 leaves Gold Standard Hosta, a yellowy green variety

6 leaves Sugar-and-Cream Hosta, a white-striped variety

6 leaves Standard Hosta, a dark green variety

1 yard green satin ribbon

Spool green florist tape

Clippers

Scissors

4 small pearl-headed pins

1. If kept cool and watered, this bouquet can be prepared the day before the wedding. Clean the chrysanthemum stems, removing all leaves. Then gather the flowers into a bunch that fits easily in your hand. Arrange into a domed shape, gently pulling up blooms at the center of the circle. To secure, wrap the stems with florist tape about three inches below the flower heads.

2. Create a collar of hosta leaves around the chrysanthemums. Holding the bouquet, begin to place leaves around the dome in a way that looks pleasing. Cluster together a few of the same leaves, and as you turn the bouquet mix in another variety of hosta, so that the end result is a layered necklace of greenery.

3. When you are happy with the placement of the leaves, tie them to the chrysanthemum bouquet with another wrap of florist tape. Start at about two inches below the leaves and tightly wrap the stems so that you end up with at least a three-inch band of tape.

4. Clip the stems of the flowers so that they are even in length. They should be about seven inches long. Immerse stems in water until ready to wrap with ribbon.

5. Wrap satin ribbon over the florist tape. Conceal the starting end under the first turn of ribbon, and continue to wrap around the stems until you've covered the tape. Wrap around once more, then cut the ribbon with sharp scissors (dull ones will fray the satin fabric). Tuck the cut edge under itself and pin into the bouquet with a row of pearl-headed pins.

Variations: Other great green flowers to consider include lady slipper and dendrobium orchids, roses, hydrangea, euphorbia, and vibernum.

fall bouquet

Sometimes it's a regal magenta singed with deep red, sometimes it's splashed with sunset orange, fiery pink, and warm yellow: No matter what the hue, dahlias always offer an exuberant profusion of painted petals. I love the bold burst of color and appreciate the robust nature of the plant. It's hardy yet plush, making it an excellent flower for bridal bouquets. Monochromatic designs are the easiest for novices to execute—the key is to incorporate contrasting textures and shapes to keep it interesting. Puffy, pumpkin-colored Japanese lantern pods are just the right accent for an autumnal bouquet, but their stems are lank, with about six blooms each, making them better suited to a vase. In order for the pods to work alongside the dahlias, I removed them from their stems and attached them instead to wire lengths.

20 Japanese lantern pods (about 6 stems, to ensure enough well-shaped pods)

20 12-inch lengths of 20-gauge green florist wire

5 large dahlias, cleaned and trimmed

½ yard yellow satin ribbon

3 pearl-headed pins

Spool green florist tape

Clippers

Scissors

3-foot strand faux grapevine

1. Clip the Japanese lantern pods from their stems, being careful not to cut the connecting sprig at each pod's base: This tiny stem will be taped to a foot-long wire stalk. Lantern pods are meant to dry, so there's no need to keep them in water.

2. Take one length of florist wire, pinch it together with one pod stem, and wrap with florist tape to bind. Pull the tape tightly, smoothing it as you go, and wind around the full length of the wire to create a flexible faux stem. Repeat for each pod.

3. Start with five stems of pods, gather into a mini bouquet, add two dahlias, arrange to please, add more lantern pods, then another dahlia. Repeat as desired. When the bouquet is complete, use florist tape to bind all the stems together.

4. Wrap satin ribbon over the tape binding to conceal. Cut the ribbon with sharp scissors (dull ones will fray the fabric), tuck the edge under itself, and anchor this folded end in place with the three pearl-headed pins.

5. Coil the wired grapevine around the stems in a loosely spaced, organic line for a finishing touch.

boutonnieres

It's a well-known fact that tuxedoed gents make women weak in the knees, and perhaps that's why boutonnieres are worn on wedding days—in case of emergency, their scent can be used to revive damsels in distress! Smart boutonnieres can be fashioned from plants you find right outside your door. Tiny pinecones and needles, rose hips, bayberry sprigs, maple leaves—any combination will work as long as the flowers are hardy by nature, since these tiny buds must make it through the day's events without water. My one plea? Keep the size diminutive: It's a boutonniere, not a corsage. Use a pearl-headed pin to anchor the flower to the lapel—the left one, of course, right over his heart.

Flowers on the stem

Foliage on the stem

4-inch stems of 24-gauge florist wire

6-inch lengths of ⅛-inch-wide satin ribbon

3-inch pearl-headed pins

Spool green florist tape

Clippers

Tissue paper

Shoe box

1. Strip flower stems of extra leaves, then wire elements as follows: Place the end of a wire stem just below the base of the flower or leaf and wrap a tight spiral of florist tape around both the wire and the plant stem to create an inch-and-a-half-long taped, wired stem. Trim the tape end.

2. Layer a stem of foliage with the blossom of your choosing. Twist selected stems together and bind with a small amount of florist tape. For the smoothest finish, pull the tape taut as you twist it in place around the stems. Florist tape has some elasticity to it, and using a small amount of tension as you wrap will ensure the best result. Tape to create an approximately two-inch-long stem and clip the end clean.

3. If desired, twist the stem into a tiny curl. Tie straight stems with a bit of satin ribbon. Select a dark color to match either the greenery or the men's suits. Insert a pearl-headed pin through the stem to await the wearer.

4. Keep floral boutonnieres fresh by making them the morning of the wedding and refrigerating until the event. Long-lasting botanicals can be made a day before. Nest them in a tissue-lined shoe box to transport them to the ceremony. And just to be on the safe side, make a few extras: Nervous hands and hearty hugs often crush small blooms.

Variations: Accent boutonniere stems with tiny satin bows, jade button rings, crystal beads, or metallic wires. Jewelry toggles can be used as teeny vases to hold boutonnieres.

floral lei

Years ago, I traveled to Hawaii on a photo shoot for *Bride's* magazine. After a long flight, we landed on the exotic Big Island. I still remember the intoxicating welcome of "aloha" and the aromatic necklace bestowed on me. The joyful symbolism of the lei makes it a charming accessory for the bridal party or a unique favor for your guests.

3 stems button chrysanthemums: yields 15 blooms

2–3 stems dendrobium orchids: yields 15 blooms

½ cup assorted color-coordinated glass beads

Spool nylon, metal, or linen bookbinder's thread

Long, sharp needle for beading, available in craft supply stores

Clippers

Tissue paper

Shoe box

1. Leaving about an inch of stem per bloom, snip the flowers off the stems.
2. For a 30-inch lei, thread the needle with a 40-inch-long piece of thread. (For longer leis, use a piece that's 10 inches longer than the desired length of the finished necklace.) Securely knot one end of the thread.
3. String a two-inch section of the thread with beads. If using more than one style or color of bead, plan to repeat the same pattern of placement for each bead section.
4. Thread one chrysanthemum bloom, followed by one orchid. The best way to spear the flowers is to insert the needle through the thick center and draw it out through the remains of the stem.
5. Repeat your pattern of beads and blooms until the thread is full. Knot ends together to create a circle.
6. Store completed leis in a tissue-lined shoe box and refrigerate, taking care not to freeze petals. Leis can be made two days in advance when using hardy flowers like chrysanthemums and orchids.

Variations: Create an all-white lei using pearl beads and white orchids, or customize the necklace with beads and flowers that match your palette. Hardy blooms like orchids and chrysanthemums, available in a wide variety of colors, make the best leis; avoid fragile, quick-to-wilt flowers. Eliminate beads and use longer lengths of string, knotting each end, to fashion floral garlands to be strewn between pews and chandelier branches, or to enshrine a ceremonial site.

basket of petals

Because flower girls are often solitary performers, they have to be brave souls, at the tender age of four or five, to walk down an aisle in a room full of strangers. I find that if you've got enough young blood in the family a flock of flower girls can be completely disarming, and it's also a more comforting arrangement for the children themselves. Flower girls may be interested to learn the origin of their role, which reads like a fairy tale: The tradition of tossing petals before the bride began centuries ago, when it was believed that a carpet of flowers protected her from demons thought to lurk in the earth below.

Small wood orchid basket, about 5 inches in diameter, available at craft shops

Drill with ⅛-inch bit

Pale moss green spray paint

2 2-inch green tassels

10-inch length of ¼-inch-wide green silk ribbon

40-inch length of 1-inch-wide green satin ribbon

Bamboo skewer

Scissors

Silk or fresh petals to fill the bucket

1. Drill one pair of holes an inch and a half apart along the rim of the basket; drill a second pair of holes directly opposite the first. These holes will be threaded with ribbon for the handles, so they need to be placed exactly opposite one another for the proper balance.

2. Spray-paint the basket in a well-ventilated area. Let dry.

3. At its halfway point, cut open the loop of cord connected to one tassel. Thread the ends of the cord through one pair of holes and tie together on the inside of the basket so that the tassel hangs on the outside. Cut the silk ribbon in half, thread it through the same pair of holes and knot together on the inside. Repeat on the opposite side of the basket.

4. Cut the satin ribbon in half. Thread one end through one of the holes: A bamboo skewer may help push the ribbon past the tassel cord. Once inserted, knot the ribbon firmly on the inside of the basket. Thread the opposite end of ribbon through the opposite hole and also knot on the inside of the basket. Repeat with the remaining half of ribbon on the opposite side of the basket, knotting the second ribbon so that it's the same length as the first handle.

5. The basket can be prepared weeks before the wedding. The morning of the wedding, fill it to the brim with petals.

rose pomander

Pint-sized cutie pies love to carry pretty flowers, and pomanders are one of my favorite arrangements for this purpose. I like the floral orbs because their ribbon loop makes them easy for small hands to handle. And the simple, pleasing shape can be created with almost any flower, to match the color scheme.

**16-inch length of
2-inch-wide satin ribbon**

**4 10-inch lengths of
organza ribbon**

**3-inch Oasis dome,
available at floral suppliers**

**4 2-inch self-wired
flower picks, available at
floral suppliers**

55 stems small roses

Clippers

Juice glasses

Tissue paper

Hat box

1. Submerge the Oasis dome in water. Remove when saturated.
2. Fold the satin ribbon in half and knot the ends securely to the plastic cage at the back of the dome. If possible, hang this satin handle on a hook or clamp over a sink or table, to create a hands-free workstation: This will prevent the flowers from getting bruised.
3. Clip the flower stems to about four inches and stand in water-filled juice glasses until ready to use. Insert stems one at a time into the Oasis dome. To help organize the arrangement, begin with a horizontal row around the circumference. Then bisect the first circle with a vertical band of flowers. This will create a cross section that can be used as a guide to ensure the even placement of flowers. As you continue to fill out the dome with the remaining roses, adjust the placement so that each blossom sits at roughly the same height.
4. Make two or three loops out of each length of organza ribbon and wire to a pick. Insert the picks around the satin ribbon handle so that the organza ribbon loops appear to emerge from this point.
5. If kept cool or refrigerated, pomanders can be made a day before the wedding. Transport to the ceremony in tissue-lined hat boxes.

feather shell satchel

Coming from a large family, I've witnessed firsthand the happiness children can bring to a wedding. Our albums are peppered with photos of smiling little faces, cockeyed curls, and fancy frocks, slightly disheveled. For a seaside reception, I used an opalescent shell to create a charming nest that held soft white feathers to be scattered by tiny hands. Instead of bridesmaids, why not be escorted by a swirl of angelic five- and six-year-olds? Children at that age love to play a starring role, and are mature enough to follow directions: They'll take the responsibility of their part in the celebration very seriously, and they'll absolutely adore the magical satchel they get to wear while walking down the aisle.

1 large nautilus-style shell: Polished versions are readily available at nautical gift shops.

2 3-inch-wide starfish

Handful of small shells like mussels and scallops

Small bag of turkey feathers, available at craft stores

1 yard white silk cord

Tape measure

Scissors

Glue gun

1. This whimsical satchel may be made weeks in advance of the celebration. Measure the child to determine the best length for the silk cord strap. The shell should hang diagonally across one shoulder and rest at about waist level. Calculate an inch at each end of the cord to be glued to the shell, and cut to fit.

2. Locate the two "dimples"—the natural depressions where the spiral begins—on the outer sides of the shell. Using the hot glue gun, apply a generous dab of glue to adhere each end of the silk cord to a dimple.

3. Hot-glue a starfish on top of one cord end to cover its raw edge. Continue by gluing a scattering of small shells around the starfish. Fill in the shell's dimpled recess with an overlapping composition that will also serve to conceal any glue dribbles. Repeat on the other side of the shell.

4. Fill the shell with small white feathers for the child to toss.

ring pillow

A sentimentalist at heart, I love to include "something borrowed" and "something blue" on the wedding day. For a bride who'd been raised by her grandmother, I fashioned a ring pillow from an embroidered lavender blue heirloom handkerchief. By having the youngest member of the family carry this pillow stitched from grandmother's linen, the past and the future came together for a most symbolic moment in the ceremony. Young ones want to please, but remember that they are still only tots, and may suffer from a last-minute bout of stage fright or hold their treasures at precarious angles. For your sake and theirs, be sure to firmly anchor the rings to the pillow with a slipknotted ribbon.

8-inch-square silk pillow, available at craft and specialty shops

8-inch-square linen handkerchief

15-inch length of ½-inch-wide satin ribbon

5 pearl beads

Needle and thread

Scissors

Sprig of rosebuds

1. Thread the needle and stitch the handkerchief to the pillow, temporarily tacking it in place with a tiny stitch and a pearl at each corner.
2. Stitch the center of the ribbon to the center of the pillow, and embellish with the final pearl. Trim ribbon ends.
3. When ready, just before the ceremony, slipknot the ribbon to anchor the rings and the sprig of rosebuds to the pillow.

Variations: Attach a brass medallion or vintage mother-of-pearl button to the center of a simple silk throw pillow to make an instant ring pillow. Stitch a cord or ribbon in place to secure your bands. And when shopping for the pillow, look for one in a hue that will live happily ever after on your bed.

Sure, dressing chairs could be considered frivolous, but it certainly looks fabulous! Even the simplest detailing on a chair back suggests that the wedding will be deliciously over the top—and all the more so if a decorative flourish graces every guest's chair. Alternately, seating accents that are limited to a select group serve to identify the guests of honor, and embellishing only the bride and groom seats is a timeless tradition. Leggy charivari ballroom chairs are my favorite. Widely available from party suppliers, these elegant seats can be rented with cushions that come in a rainbow of different colors. Many suppliers will also paint the chairs a custom shade for an additional fee. The sleek physique of the ballroom chair makes it easier to fit an extra person at each table, and the lattice back accommodates everything from floral garlands to silken bows. Best of all, ballroom chairs also look great au naturel.

woven ribbon skirt

Luxurious notions inspire me, and I find it impossible to come away from passementerie stores without a yard or two of some fabulous trim to experiment with. Yet, the classic satin ribbon remains my creative staple. Available in every color under the sun, the silky strands invite touch. To skirt ballroom chairs with a sensuous fringe, simply weave the ribbons together.

½ yard kraft paper, to make template

19 65-inch lengths of 2-inch-wide satin ribbon; mix colors if desired

Tape measure

Pencil

Scissors

Roll clear 3-inch packing tape

Ballroom chair, with basic white cushion

4 1-inch Velcro buttons

1. On the kraft paper, trace the chair seat you wish to cover. Cut out this pattern to use as a template.

2. Plan to work with the shiny surface of the ribbon facing down. Tape the kraft-paper template to a worktable. Measure in 25 inches from the end of one ribbon and line up with the left vertical edge of the template. Lay the ribbon across the top of the template and temporarily tape in place. Using the first ribbon as a guide, repeat to cover the template with horizontal stripes.

3. Weave ribbons vertically, over and then under the horizontally placed ribbons. Once again mark 25 inches from the end of a ribbon and line this up with the bottom edge of the template. Then start weaving, threading the ribbon over and under all the horizontal ribbons. Pull the ribbon taut as you weave it, and be sure it lines up along the edge of the template. Temporarily tape this first vertical ribbon in place with a bit of clear packing tape. Repeat with a second ribbon, but alternate the weave by threading it *under* the first horizontal ribbon, *over* the second horizontal ribbon and so on to the end of the horizontal ribbons. When all the ribbons have been woven together, adjust as necessary to make a smooth seat.

4. Secure the weave with clear packing tape. Begin at the upper left-hand corner of the underside of the weave and tape diagonally, to the lower right-hand corner. Repeat for the other two corners to form an X. Smooth tape in place. Then tape around the perimeter. The tape should not extend beyond the edges of the template.

5. Flip over to place on the chair seat. Adhere a Velcro button at each corner to affix the skirt to the chair.

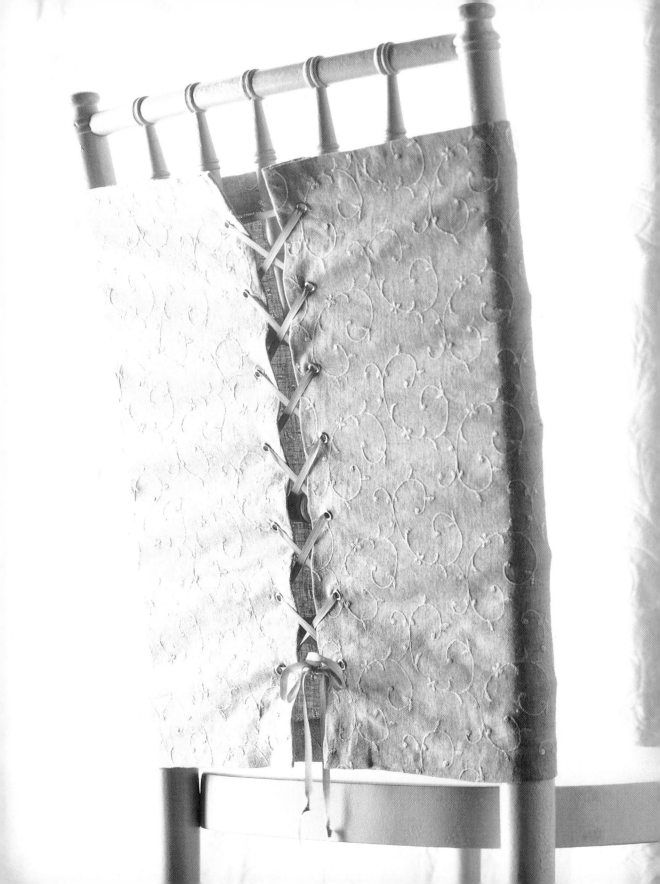

corset slipcover

Tradition with a twist: Embroidered muslin laced with ribbon brings just a bit of sexiness to ballroom chair backs. This barely brazen garb is best suited to receptions. Corset styles would be out of place in religious atmospheres. When in doubt, simple slipcovers are a safe bet. And although extravagant celebrants might want to dress every chaise in fancy duds, if you choose to seat guests in ballroom chairs at the ceremony, a more visually effective option would be to decorate only the backs of those chairs that line the aisles. You'll discover that the elegant silhouette of this seat looks just as graceful when simply adorned.

⅔ yard of favorite fabric

Roll ½-inch-wide adhesive webbing for fabric seams

Grommet kit containing ⅛-inch grommet tool and 15-20 grommet rings, available at hardware stores

2 yards of ⅛-inch-wide satin ribbon, to lace the corset

Tape measure

Pinking shears

Scissors

Tailor's chalk

Iron

1. Measure the height and width of the chair back. Double the width, then add two inches to both the doubled width and to the height: This will allow for a one-inch seam all around the perimeter of the fabric. Cut the fabric with pinking shears, to prevent fraying.
2. With scissors, cut enough six-inch sections of adhesive webbing to seam the fabric. To estimate the number of sections needed, measure the perimeter of the fabric, then divide by six. Set sections aside.
3. Iron a one-inch-deep fold around the perimeter of the fabric. Then insert one section of adhesive webbing between the fabric and the fold, and press in place. The heat from the iron will melt the webbing and create a quick bond for the hem. Repeat to bond the entire hem. At each corner, take care to fold the fabric neatly into a flat, triangular pleat before pressing in place.
4. Mark the placement points for the grommet holes with tailor's chalk or a pen. The holes should be spaced equally, with the first and last hole for each row resting at least an inch and a half from the horizontal edge of the fabric.
5. Follow the directions on the package to create grommet holes. Basically, you'll be punching the fabric to make holes that are sealed with protective metal rings.
6. Lace the corset slipcover to the chair with thin satin ribbon, and tie tiny love knots into the ends.

silk flower garland

Formal fetes call for dressing to the nines, chairs included. When decorating furniture, silk flowers are especially easy to use. Their wire stems make them a crafts staple, and, of course, they afford you the benefit of time, since they can be styled weeks in advance of the wedding. All silk flowers, however, are not created equal. I personally prefer vintage millinery samples. I often find boxes of unusual fabric blooms at my favorite flea markets, and their distinctive designs make them highly desirable collectibles.

3-foot length of faux grapevine

1 large silk camellia, about 4 inches in diameter

3 medium white silk roses, about 2½ inches in diameter

5 small white silk roses, about 1 inch in diameter

3 small pink silk roses

2 small green silk roses

2 beaded tassels

Spool green florist tape

Scissors

1. Mentally divide the faux grapevine into three sections. Plan to reserve 10 inches at each end of the vine to be used to attach the finished garland to the chair back.

2. Line up the silk flowers on a worktable and experiment with their placement. Group the flowers close together, with the largest blooms at the center. To create a lush garland, I made a camellia the focal point and surrounded it with roses in various sizes and shades.

3. When satisfied with your arrangement, wire the flowers to the grapevine. Starting at the center and working outward, twist the flower stems into the vine and wrap with florist tape to attach. Work with the tape on the spool, stretching and shaping it as you go. Tightly wind tape around each stem to secure the flower, then nestle another flower next to it and tape in place. Repeat until all the flowers are attached.

4. Once all the flowers have been taped in place, attach a beaded tassel to each end of the garland. It's easy to fasten the tassels with a few twists of the wired vine.

5. Position the garland along the chair back, utilizing the reserved inches of vine to affix it. For a finishing touch, curl the ends so that they resemble the tendrils of real grapevines.

double-face bows

Imagine waltzing into a reception room where the tables are covered with luxe skirts of celadon silk and the cushioned ballroom chairs are cinched with plush bows of crisp celery and blazing pink. Smartly tailored threads always make a grand impression. Sewn from two long panels of fabric, double-face silk bows make simple but equally elegant alternatives to classic chair slipcovers. I prefer to use two different but complementary colors. Once wrapped and tied, each chair looks like a fabulous gift.

10 x 100-inch length of celadon silk

10 x 100-inch length of hot pink silk

Straight pins

Sewing machine

Scissors

Bone folder

Iron

Needle and thread

1. Layer the two pieces of silk face-to-face, with the preferred side of each fabric facing inward.
2. Pin the two pieces of silk together along the perimeter. Insert pins perpendicularly into the fabric, and space them about two inches apart.
3. Sew the two pieces of silk together along the perimeter, placing the seam one-half of an inch in from the edge of the fabric. Remove the pins as you sew. Leave a five-inch gap between the end and the beginning of the seam.
4. Use scissors to clip a half-inch notch into each of the four corners of the fabric. The notches should not cut through the seam.
5. Gently turn the case inside out, pulling the correct face of the fabric through the five-inch opening. Poke the fabric flat in each corner by inserting the tip of the bone folder through the opening.
6. With the iron on a low setting, lightly press the finished case to flatten the seams.
7. Use a needle and thread to stitch closed the five-inch opening.
8. Tie a bow to each chair. The predominant color should face out when encircling the chair back. Pull the fabric tightly and knot around the chair ribs.

Variations: If you find yourself pressed for time, tailors and seamstresses can also provide sewing services for this easy project. Or use four-inch-wide satin ribbon to tie basic but beautiful bows around the chair backs.

Country fresh, sleek and sophisticated, charming or whimsical, centerpieces can express many moods. Your choice should fit the location and the overall style of your wedding. A well-designed centerpiece must reflect the formality and complement the color palette of your event, and, of course, lush blooms will never go out of style, but I suggest you think beyond the basic flowers-in-a-glass-vase for inspiration. Consider some of my favorite objects: Gilded nuts, a pile of pearls, waxy fruits, colored water, vintage holiday ornaments, and antique birdcages all make more imaginative centerpieces. Take time to create a look that will seduce guests, because successful centerpieces are more than mere decoration, they are a form of entertainment that makes a big statement, silently. Whatever style you select, remember: Fresh looks best. Be sure to arrange cut flowers no more than two days before the wedding.

mixed apple centerpiece

Budgets for weddings can add up, and to save money it's often necessary to simplify details, but sacrificing style for savings is never an option in my book. For dramatic centerpieces at a fraction of the cost of floral arrangements I always suggest seasonal vegetables and fruits. Farmers' markets or produce aisles offer bushels of affordable picks. For a fall table, fill tall glass hurricanes to the brim with a mix of crisp orchard fruits, and serve sparkling ciders to continue the spirit of the season.

18-inch glass hurricane

3 pounds mixed apples

1. Fill the hurricane with rinsed and polished apples. Stagger the sizes for a more interesting arrangement, and fill any gaps with the smaller apples. This centerpiece can easily be made up to four days before the wedding.

Variations: Colorful citrus fruits, pears, cherries, grapes, nuts, and peppers are all excellent components for centerpieces. Fill rustic market baskets, carved hardwood bowls, square glass vases, antique cake plates, and galvanized platters with piles of vibrant produce. For a dressier variation on simple fruit in a bowl, brush the fruit with egg white and roll in granulated sugar. But note: This should be done no more than a day in advance.

three tiers of flowers

Inspired by the unmistakable shape of a stacked cake, I gave a fresh spin to the traditional floral design technique of grouping together similar blooms when I layered three different flowers in complementary colors one on top of another. The result is an exuberant silhouette that echoes the lines of a classic wedding cake.

30 stems sweet pea

8 stems lilac

5 heads hydrangea

3 4 x 4 x 6-inch Oasis bricks, available at florist suppliers

Florist knife

Florist clay

Clippers

Ruler

Roll ¼-inch-wide waterproof florist tape

8-inch-round glass saucer

10-inch-round cake pedestal

1. With the florist knife, cut one of the Oasis bricks to 3 x 4 x 6 inches. Immerse all the bricks in water until saturated, about 20 minutes. Place one full-sized brick and the trimmed brick within the glass saucer, trimming further if necessary to fit both bricks side by side. Be sure to line up the bricks so that they are level. Oasis arrangements should be made no more than one day in advance.

2. Trim the remaining brick into a four-inch cube. Stack the cube on top of the first layer of Oasis bricks. Use six 20-inch strips of florist tape applied in a crisscross pattern to attach the foam to the saucer.

3. Use a wad of florist clay about the size of a half dollar to anchor the bottom of the saucer to the top of the pedestal.

4. Clip the hydrangea stems to about eight inches long. Insert about three inches of each stem into the base of the Oasis, encircling it with a ruff of petals. Be careful not to poke too many trial-and-error placement holes into the Oasis, because the foam will crumble if it becomes too honeycombed.

5. Clip the lilac stems four inches longer than the panicles and insert each stem deep into the midsection of the Oasis to create the second ring of flowers. If necessary, further trim the lilac stems so that this layer looks narrower than the hydrangea layer.

6. Clip half of the sweet pea stems to four inches and insert into the Oasis to create the third ring of flowers. Clip the remaining sweet pea stems to six inches and insert these taller lengths into the top center of the Oasis to give the arrangement its height.

7. Carefully tug and adjust the stems as necessary to emphasize the triangular, tiered shape of the arrangement.

acrylic troughs

One of my favorite materials to work with is acrylic. This versatile plastic comes in many colors and can be cut into different shapes to create all kinds of decorative objects. I've used acrylic to make trays and columns, screens and containers. Plastic suppliers will cut acrylic to order, and can also fabricate containers and structures to your specifications. However, it's less expensive and very easy to use acrylic adhesive, known as solvent, to piece together your own designs. I crafted transparent troughs from half-inch-thick frosted acrylic panels, then filled the elongated containers with wheat grass and miniature daffodils. For a springtime ceremony, what could be more cheerful?

Acrylic solvent with application syringe

3 x 33-inch panel of ½-inch-thick frosted acrylic, for the base

2 2½ x 33-inch panels of ½-inch-thick frosted acrylic, for the long sides

2 2 x 2½-inch panels of ½-inch-thick frosted acrylic, for the short sides

10 x 20-inch flat of wheat grass, available at health food stores and farmers' markets

3 6-inch plastic pots of miniature daffodils, available at plant nurseries in season

Utility knife

Ruler

Bamboo skewer

1. Fill the application syringe with acrylic solvent.
2. Situate the base panel on your worktable. Take one of the long side panels and squirt solvent along its bottom edge. Place the long side panel on top of the base, aligning the edges and ends, and hold in place until secure. Acrylic solvent will dry in just a few minutes. Repeat on the other side with the other long panel.
3. To complete the trough, squirt solvent along the bottom edge of each short side panel and insert in place. Let dry.
4. No more than two days before the wedding, trim the flat of wheat grass with the utility knife so that you have a 2½ x 20-inch strip. Then cut a 2½ x 12-inch strip from the remaining grass so that, when aligned, the two strips extend 32 inches—the length of the trough. Press the strips into the trough, using your fingertips to fill the corners and edges. The grass should fit snugly.
5. Separate the potted daffodils into individual bulbs. Use the bamboo skewers to poke holes in the wheat grass and replant individual flowers in the trough. Place them randomly, for a natural, field-grown presentation. Water to keep moist.

Variations: Acrylic troughs make excellent containers for tea lights. The geometric box keeps these myriad little candles in place, and the transparent material enhances the flames' glow.

blooming birdcage

Flea markets are my favorite place to find unusual objects to be used as centerpieces. At one I frequent often, I found a pair of wire birdcages. Immediately, I pictured them filled with sunny daffodils and vivid wheat grass. Admittedly, it took a few months of prowling flea markets and on-line auctions before I turned up enough birdcages so that each table at the reception could be graced with one, but because most couples are engaged for more than six months, there's certainly time to track down such treasures.

White wired birdcage, 12 inches tall with an 8-inch-round base

8½-inch-round saucer

10-inch-round charger plate

18 stems miniature daffodils

18 2-inch floral water tubes, also often known as aqua picks, available from floral suppliers

8-inch round of wheat grass, available at health food stores and farmers' markets

3 bunches baby parsley or other small-leaved green

Sprig variegated ivy

Florist knife

Florist clay

Bamboo skewer (optional)

Wired feather butterfly, available at craft and floral suppliers

1. Temporarily bond the saucer to the charger with a quarter-sized wad of florist clay. Place the clay on the bottom center of the saucer and squish the two plates together to hold.
2. Nest the birdcage in the saucer, using several small wads of florist clay to anchor it in place. Plan to fill with flowers and foilage no more than two days before the wedding.
3. Through the opening in the birdcage (depending on your finds, some will have side doors, others flip tops), fit in the round of wheat grass so that it completely covers the bottom. If necessary, use the florist knife to cut the sod into sections that will fit through the opening, then reassemble the round once it is inside the cage. Use fingers or a bamboo skewer to fluff the blades and conceal any cuts in the sod.
4. Uncap the tubes, fill with water, recap, and insert a daffodil in each one.
5. Spear each tube into the sod in a random pattern to create a miniature flowering meadow.
6. Ring the cage with baby parsley to conceal the sod's edges.
7. Twist the wired stem of the feather butterfly either around a daffodil stem or to the cage itself. At the top of the cage, entwine the sprig of ivy.

gilded tree

On a recent trek through a flower market, I spotted the stark yet graceful silhouette of a manzanita branch and decided to use it to create a chic centerpiece. An ornamental brass lighting plate I'd found at a flea market became the base of my miniature tree, and bits of gold leaf gilded the branches. For the tree's blooms, I selected roses, which hold up well without water. Branches both natural and manufactured are readily available from purveyors of dried flowers and foliage—I've even seen manzanita sold at pet stores as bird perches. Look for branches that unfurl like shapely shade trees.

18-inch-tall manzanita branch with a horizontal span of 24 inches

10 roses

12 sheets of 4-inch-square faux gold leaf, available at art supply stores

Ornamental brass ceiling light fixture plate, about 6 inches in diameter, available at lighting supply stores and flea markets

Spray adhesive

2 sheets newspaper

Masking tape

Florist glue

⅞-inch furniture bolt set, available at hardware stores

⅞-inch butterfly bolt, available at hardware stores

Screwdriver

Drill

Hacksaw

Clippers

1. Use the hacksaw to cut a flat base across the end of the branch. Drill a one-inch hole into the base, then thread the female half of the furniture bolt into this hole. Insert the male end of the furniture bolt into the female with the screwdriver. One inch of the screw should emerge from the base of the branch.

2. Thread the brass plate over the screw and anchor it in place with the butterfly bolt so that the flat side of the brass plate rests on the table. To protect the plate from spray adhesive, temporarily cover it with some old newspaper held in place with masking tape.

3. In a well-ventilated workroom, spritz the branch with spray adhesive. Do not coat the entire branch. The adhesive will be used to attach gold leaf to the branch, and since parts of the natural bark should remain exposed, it's important not to gild the whole branch. The gold leaf will stick to sprayed sections only.

4. Handle the gold leaf gingerly, and apply one sheet at a time. Wrap the sticky sections of the branch with a square of gold leaf, rubbing it on with your fingertips. Use all remaining fragments of gold leaf to detail the branch, rubbing on bits and pieces until it's covered as desired. Trees may be made weeks in advance to this point.

5. The morning of the event, prepare the flowers. Select long-lasting varieties like well-hydrated roses and orchids. Cut the flower heads at the base, then use florist glue to attach each bloom to the branch. Keep the finished arrangement in a refrigerated or air-conditioned space until ready to set the tables.

dahlia centerpiece

Inspiration strikes at unlikely moments. One day as I was admiring a simple glass ice bucket it occurred to me that to creatively conceal the stems of arranged blooms, the container itself could be filled with flower heads. Experimenting with a lush bunch of dahlias, I discovered that the exuberant blossoms became a delightful, Impressionistic splash of paint when submerged. Topping the underwater flower heads with a fluffy bouquet of even more dahlias completed the colorful masterpiece.

1 bunch long-stemmed dahlias plus 17 additional flower heads to submerge

Glass ice bucket

Narrow glass cylinder, the same height as the ice bucket

Bamboo skewer

1. Clean the stems of the dahlias, removing all but the first few leaves below each bloom. Select the largest blooms for the arrangement, trim an inch off their stems, and place them in water. From the remaining flowers—I used 17—cut the heads off the stems and set aside.

2. Center the narrow cylinder inside the ice bucket. Fill both with water.

3. Insert flower heads one by one in the space between the cylinder and the ice bucket. The flower heads should face out. Use the bamboo skewer to fluff and style the petals of each bloom. Repeat until the entire bucket is full.

4. Arrange the long-stemmed dahlias in the cylinder the day before the wedding.

Variations: Sliced lemons or limes, cranberries, grapes, peppers, even spears of asparagus—all are excellent submersibles. Vibrant produce makes the strongest impact: Contrast colors for a whimsical pairing or match the hue of the flowers for a more formal presentation.

strawberry topiary

Often described as the favored fruit of lovers, strawberries add sweetness to frothy cocktails, succulent custard tarts, even dark green salads. And when a shipping error left an extra gross of almost ripe berries on my doorstep, I found one more use for the fruit, transforming the bounty into bacchanalian centerpieces. Colorful and fragrant, the berry topiaries are an alternative to traditional floral arrangements, but must be made no earlier than the day before the wedding.

1 flat (about 8 quarts) of large, almost ripe Driscoll strawberries

6 branches lemon leaf: each yields about 5 leaves

8-inch square of wheat grass, available at health food stores and farmers' markets

5-inch green Styrofoam ball, available at floral suppliers

3 17-inch-long, 1-inch-round bamboo sticks, available at garden centers

1 pint bag quick-dry concrete, available at hardware stores

6-inch-deep decorative ceramic or terra-cotta pot

4-inch-deep plastic container sized to fit snugly inside the pot

Package 4-inch-long bamboo skewers

Spool florist wire

Box straight pins

Utility knife

1. Bind the three bamboo sticks together using florist wire. Two inches from each end, wrap the wire twice around the sticks. Twist ends together to secure.
2. With the bamboo bundle and plastic container on hand, prepare the concrete according to the package instructions. Pour into the plastic container and stand the bamboo bundle in the middle of the mix. Hold in place until concrete stiffens, about five minutes.
3. Center the Styrofoam ball over the exposed ends of the bamboo. Using slight pressure, push the ball into the sticks to a depth of two inches.
4. Pin lemon leaves to the base of the ball to create a verdant collar around the bamboo.
5. Insert one end of a bamboo skewer one inch deep into the broad base of each berry, handling gently to prevent bruising. Insert the opposite end into the ball. Insert berries in a pleasingly compact arrangement, but don't be too concerned about following a strict pattern: The berries should look like they're blooming naturally from the ball.
6. Once the ball is covered with strawberries, pin on more lemon leaves to conceal gaps and give the topiary an organic finish.
7. Place the plastic container in the decorative pot. Cut the wheat grass square in half. Wrap each half around the base of the bamboo to conceal the concrete, pushing the sod into the pot with your fingertips. Further trim the sod as necessary to fit. Fluff the blades of grass; mist to keep fresh. The topiary can be refrigerated overnight, but always handle it with care, because bruised or overripe berries may bleed.

pinecone centerpiece

Metallic accents make holiday tables sparkle—the reflective surfaces seem to dance in the candlelight. I love to give winter receptions an elegant gleam by layering tables with lots of gilded and silver elements: gold-rimmed china, shiny satin napkin ribbons, place cards scripted in glittering ink. For centerpieces, I often employ fleets of silver candlesticks or sterling Revere bowls filled with floating roses. But when I want to make a big, glossy splash I grab a can of spray paint and go to town, covering walnut shells and pinecones with a coat of silver. When piled into a large, wide mercury glass, they create a centerpiece that's affordably sumptuous.

20 medium pinecones

20 petite pinecones

1 pound bag of walnuts

Can metallic silver spray paint

2-foot-deep cardboard box

2–3 paper bags or sheets of kraft paper to use as a drying surface

Plastic bags for storage

Large mercury glass or silver bowl

1. In a well-ventilated room or garage, empty the bag of walnuts into the cardboard box. Spray with silver paint, shake the box to toss, then spray again as needed to coat the nuts.

2. Tear open the paper bags or lay out the sheets of kraft paper and spill the painted nuts onto them to dry.

3. Repeat steps 1 and 2 with the pinecones.

4. Once dry, store the spray-painted nuts and pinecones in plastic bags until ready to use. Because nuts and pinecones are nonperishable, they can be painted weeks, even months, before the wedding.

5. Fill the bowl to the brim with a salad of silver nuts and pinecones.

Variations: Spray paints are available in silver, gold, and copper. For a metallic medley, use two shades, spraying the nuts one color and the pinecones another. Branches and evergreen foliage also look fabulous painted: Use quick spurts instead of steady streams of paint so that the foliage appears dusted with shine rather than lacquered with color.

rock sugar centerpiece

If a little color goes a long way, then a lot of color makes a real splash! I love to set tables in bright shades because they always cause a stir. Wildly striped linens instantly add energy to the room, and ballroom chairs can be rented in matching lipstick hues. The key is to work with colors of equal intensity: hot pink, cherry red, vivid violet, and sunny orange. To complete this spicy-sweet tableau, I filled glass compotes with pink rock sugar, then nestled candy-striped pillar candles in the granules.

8½ x 11-inch sheet of vellum printed with the couple's names and wedding date

Paper cutter

Glue stick

Pink-striped pillar candle, 6 inches tall, 4 inches round

8-inch-round glass compote (a shallow bowl on a pedestal)

1 quart pink rock sugar, available from confectionery suppliers

1. With the paper cutter, trim the printed vellum into strips. One standard-sized sheet can be used to create five 1½ x 8-inch strips.
2. Wrap a strip of vellum just above the base of the pillar candle and secure with a little glue.
3. Fill the compote with rock sugar and nestle the pillar candle in the center.

Variations: To create a lollipop centerpiece for children's tables, anchor a small dome of Oasis foam to the center of the compote or cake plate with a small wad of florist clay, insert lollipops into the dome, then cover it with rock sugar. Look for translucent candy discs in a rainbow of colors, cheerfully wrapped bubble-gum pops, or classic striped swirls the size of saucers.

pearl centerpiece

What makes a perfect centerpiece? An arrangement that feels festive but doesn't obscure the view between guests seated at the table. I love clear vases filled with beads or pearls to conceal flower stems. Baubles instantly dress up Mother Nature's efflorescence, making this a very simple yet elegant look for wedding tables.

30 stems paper white narcissus

3 cups plastic pearls

4-inch metal frog

Florist clay

Footed, clear glass cylindrical vase with an 8-inch mouth

1. Center the frog at the bottom of the vase and anchor it in place with a quarter-sized wad of florist clay.
2. Anchor the narcissus stems in the frog. Cluster the flowers together to create a lush arrangement.
3. Pour the plastic pearls around the stems to fill the vase.
4. Add three inches of cool, clear water to keep the flowers hydrated, and be sure to make this arrangement no more than two days before the celebration.

Variations: It's easy to customize this design to complement your color palette. Instead of pearls, try marbles, fragments of sea glass, or cranberries, then select favorite flowers to match.

blue water bowls

The most tranquil moments of my life have been spent by the water, and I've often looked to the sea for inspiration. So it occurred to me that a row of simple, shallow glass bowls could be transformed into a dramatic centerpiece with nothing more than water, a few drops of food coloring, and a floating candle or two. The effect is hypnotic, as if a soothing, sparkling river is running right through the table.

6 shallow, 4-inch-square glass vases

12 cups tap water

10 small, round floating candles

Blue food coloring

Bamboo skewer

4 handfuls tumbled glass stones, available from craft suppliers

1. Fill vases with water—shallow containers will need about two cups each. Add at least four drops of food coloring per vase and stir with the bamboo skewer to create a deep blue hue.
2. Line up the vases in a row, then scatter the candles down the line to create a river of light. Alternately, for round or square tables, arrange vases in a grid pattern.
3. Scatter handfuls of tumbled glass stones at different points down the row of vases.

Variations: Glass containers of any size can be filled with water in any color to complement your scheme. Just experiment in advance for the best ratio of water to food coloring per container. In addition to candles, float starry stephanotis or water hyacinth blossoms.

zen centerpiece

Creative centerpieces help define the mood of a wedding. For a couple enamored of the contemplative aesthetic of Asian cultures, I suggested a centerpiece that's best described as a serene landscape. This miniature rock garden of beach stones, tea lights, and celadon button chrysanthemums is a snap to construct and is easy to personalize.

18-inch-square copper tray, available at garden supply centers

2 dry quarts river gravel, available at tropical fish stores

12 tea lights

4 stems chrysanthemum: yields about 30 blooms

Clippers

3-inch length of 22-gauge copper wire

2 24-inch-long wired faux bamboo stems, available at silk flower suppliers

1. Pour river gravel into the copper tray. Fill to a depth of one inch.

2. Nest tea lights in the gravel. Scatter them in a random arrangement.

3. Clip flower heads to separate them from their stems. Insert faceup in the gravel. (Chrysanthemums are long-lasting blooms and will hold up easily without water for a day.)

4. Insert one end of a wired faux bamboo stem into one corner of the tray, arc it over the arrangement, and insert the other end into the corner diagonally opposite. Insert the remaining bamboo stem into the other two tray corners. Connect the two stems at the top center of their arcs with a twist of copper wire.

Variations: Use sand instead of gravel to create a beach scene. Small shells also work well. If the tray is watertight, combine stones and floating flowers to create a calming miniature pool.

table numbers, escort & place cards

A well-dressed table layers color and texture to create an inviting oasis, but a successful reception relies on more than pretty place settings to greet guests. Savvy event planners know the value of traffic control, and the reality of most receptions is that guests need to be guided to their seats. But practical solutions should never be boring. If you arrange seating—a gesture I always recommend for receptions where a meal will be served—you'll want to employ escort cards to direct each guest to the appropriate table. In fact, the escort card station is often the first design element that guests encounter. Easy-to-read numbers—or names, a playful and increasingly popular alternative—draw guests' attention to their individual tables. And once at the table, guests look for place cards to locate their seat. Each of these hardworking components presents an opportunity to instill your décor with wit and style.

escort card tree

An imaginative escort card station is a lively addition to the décor of any reception. For a winter wedding, I bedecked an evergreen with crystal ornaments and cards embellished with metal stars. This tabletop spruce comfortably extended cards to 20 couples. For larger weddings, consider using a full-grown tree, and vary your foliage and ornaments to suit the season. I always suggest that couples consider situating escort card stations wherever they plan to serve cocktails. This helps eliminate the bottleneck that results when too many people approach an escort card table located near the entrance to the dining hall. Arrange the cards in alphabetical order and, if possible, assign a server to the station. Arm this concierge with decorative scissors so that he or she can quickly snip cards from the tree.

3-foot-tall spruce tree

40 wired crystal drops, available at craft stores

2 x 3-inch escort card with envelope per couple

Calligraphy or metallic markers

Box of metal stars, available at craft stores

Glue

¹⁄₁₆-inch hole punch

Spool 22-gauge silver wire, cut into 1 4-inch length per card

1 quart bag quick-dry concrete, available at hardware stores

Silver ice bucket

Plastic tub sized to fit snugly inside the ice bucket

2 yards heavy-duty tinfoil

1 pound large silver dragées

1. Prepare the escort cards and label the envelopes with the guests' names using a calligraphy or metallic marker. Adhere a star to the front of each envelope with a dot of glue. Punch a hole at the top center and thread it with a length of silver wire, which will be used to hang each envelope from the tree.

2. The day before the event, with the tree and the plastic tub on hand, prepare the quick-dry concrete according to the package instructions. Immediately pour into the plastic tub and stand the tree in the center of the mix. Be sure the tree is straight, and hold the trunk firmly in place: The concrete hardens quickly. When dry, its weight will stabilize the centerpiece. Carefully place the plastic tub into the ice bucket.

3. Crunch and tuck tinfoil around the trunk to conceal the plastic tub and the concrete, and to create a reflective apron beneath the branches.

4. Hang crystal drops from the tree. Scatter them randomly between the branches.

5. Hang the wired envelopes from top to bottom in alphabetical order, but place the bride and broom's cards together at the very top of the tree.

6. Sprinkle silver dragées over the tinfoil at the base of the tree.

escort card table

Tent cards work well on traditional escort card tables: Compared to envelopes, these little paper pyramids bring some dimension to a flat surface, and arranged alphabetically they make it easier for guests to spot their names. Packages of blank folds in a variety of papers are widely available from stationers, and it's also simple to cut your own cards from heavy stock. Each guest or couple to be seated together should receive an individually lettered card, with their complete name on the front and the table number on the inside. Although guests won't linger long at the table, I still like to dress it with a welcoming centerpiece, such as this warm bouquet of lilies and narcissus.

40 stems yellow narcissus

**10 stems miniature
yellow calla lilies**

3-inch metal frog

½-yard florist tape

1 yard wired ribbon

3 pearl-headed pins

Clippers

Florist clay

Shallow bowl

1. Center the frog at the bottom of the bowl and anchor it in place with a quarter-sized wad of florist clay.
2. Mix the narcissus and calla lilies into a lively bouquet. Gather the stems in one hand and style with the other, gently tugging up stems at the center so that the bouquet has a domed shape. Wrap stems with florist tape a few inches below the flower heads to secure the arrangement.
3. Conceal the florist tape with ribbon. Start wrapping about two inches below the flower heads, and fold the last 10 inches of ribbon into a simple bow to create a smart, tailored collar for the bouquet. Affix the ribbon with a row of pearl-headed pins.
4. Gently pull the stems apart a bit so that the base of the bouquet flares out. Clip the stems to create a uniform flat edge. Press the stems into the frog to anchor the bouquet in the bowl. Add an inch or two of cool, clear water to keep the flowers hydrated.

Mrs.
Anne Frazier
Mr. and Mrs.
Mr. and Mrs.
Farrell
Mr. and Mrs.
Mr.
David English
Mrs.
Dorothy Jaffe

escort card curtain

In the seventies, capiz curtains were all the rage, popular as room dividers and screens for open entryways. Whenever a visitor walked through the long strands of iridescent shells, they'd chime pleasingly upon contact. Naturally opalescent, the shells are often dyed different colors, then sold in sets of 15 on six-foot strands of nylon line. For novel escort "cards," I decided to letter a couple of capiz shell curtains. Logically, names should be arranged in alphabetical order. Depending on the size of your guest list, you might want to assign one strand of shells for each letter of the alphabet. Work out the details on paper before inking the shells, then experiment with your writing technique on a practice strand.

2 sets of capiz curtains in the color of your choice, available at party supply stores

Metallic marker

Tension rod, ½ inch in diameter

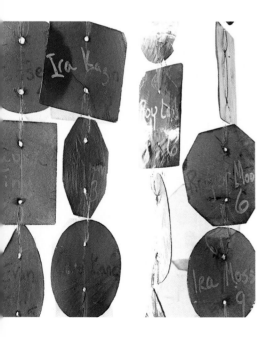

1. Allow one strand of shells to practice writing names and numbers. Capiz shells have a textured surface, so it's best to letter them with markers. Snip off and discard the practice strand once you've perfected your technique.
2. Since each strand is six feet long, begin lettering about 10 inches from the top—eye level for the average person. List names alphabetically, and allow plenty of time to letter and number the shells.
3. Hang the curtains from a tension rod at the entrance to the reception area.

cherry blossom escort cards

In the quest to create a memorable event, it's as easy to err on the side of simplicity as it is to err with excess. True, too many elements may overwhelm, but too few can be plain boring. My solution? Layer simply styled elements to achieve the optimum degree of design. From a horizontally hung lattice flat I suspended a small forest of pink paper discs, then centered a large glass filled with flowering cherry branches on the table below. I cannot tell a lie: It took everybody's breath away. With a small pair of scissors, two servers clipped cards from the ribbons and handed them to the guests as they arrived.

8½ x 11-inch sheets of paper card stock: 1 sheet yields 4 cards

Paper cutter

Disc cutter, available at craft stores

⅛-inch hole punch

Pink ink calligraphy marker

2-foot length of ½-inch-wide ribbon per card

Wired paper leaves, 1 per card

3 x 5-foot lattice flat, available at home and garden centers

Drill with plastic bit

4 circle-end ½-inch bolts

Spool 30-pound monofilament plastic thread

4 small hooks (optional)

1. Use the paper cutter to divide each sheet of card stock into four squares. Then use the disc cutter to cut three-inch circles from each square. Punch a single hole a half-inch from the top of each disc.

2. In the center of each disc, under the punched hole, write a guest's name and table number with the calligraphy marker.

3. Knot and bow one end of a ribbon length through the punched hole in each disc. Thread the stem of a paper leaf through the hole and wire it to the ribbon at the back side of the card to secure.

4. Drill a hole to fit a circle bolt in each corner of the lattice flat, then twist circle bolts in place. Knot equal lengths of monofilament to each bolt and suspend the lattice flat from ceiling pipes (found frequently in loftlike environments) or other stable fixtures. If necessary, drill four small hooks where needed into the ceiling for this purpose. The lattice flat should hang at least seven feet above the floor.

5. Arrange the cards in alphabetical order and tie them to the lattice flat, staggering the lengths to help with legibility. The flat will accommodate 150 cards.

Variations: To create an indoor gazebo, spray-paint the lattice white and use wads of florist clay to position it on top of four eight-foot-tall white pillars, available to rent from party suppliers.

escort card confetti boxes

Versatile and modern, transparent plastic has become one of my favorite decorative materials, and today it's available at art supply stores in many colors and sizes. These tinted three-inch rounds made perfect containers for glittering confetti, and they turned out to be quite easy to letter. A few strokes of metallic marker transformed them into contemporary escort cards.

**3-inch lidded plastic box
 per guest**

¼ cup confetti per box

Metallic markers

1. Use metallic markers to letter each lid with a guest's name and table number.
2. Fill each box with a handful of confetti.
3. Put the lids back on and display the boxes alphabetically.

Variations: When the bride and groom make their exit at the end of the evening, guests can shower them with the confetti from their boxes. Or fill the boxes with sweets, votive candles, or perhaps a commemorative ornament and the escort boxes can double as favors. To turn the boxes into place cards, leave off the numbers and situate the lettered containers at table settings.

table number bucket

When it comes to seating guests efficiently, nothing beats an easily identifiable table number. But nothing detracts from a well-dressed table like a number that does not complement the décor. I look for charming ways to simultaneously expose and camouflage this practical necessity—for example, by displaying the number on a centerpiece container. This double-duty design saves money and demonstrates your creativity.

Enamel-finished decorative bucket

Glue gun

Printed contact paper, or printed vellum and spray adhesive

Number stencils

Pencil

Scissors

Bunch of flowers to match bucket's color

1. Fill the bucket with water to test for leaks and seepage, since manufactured buckets are not always watertight. If necessary, draw a continuous bead of hot glue over the seam at the base of the inside of the bucket to seal.

2. Stencil the table number on the reverse side of a sheet of printed contact paper, or on either side of a sheet of printed vellum. Cut out.

3. If using contact paper, crack and peel the number from its backing and center it under the handle where it connects to the bucket. Place contact paper carefully: Once attached, it's difficult to reposition. If using printed vellum, spray the reverse side of the number with adhesive, following the directions on the can, then stick the number onto the bucket. These adhesives aren't permanent, so it's easy enough to readjust to correct positioning errors.

4. Fill the numbered bucket with a bunch of daffodils or other cheerful flowers and add water.

Variations: Instead of using numbers, distinguish one table from another with different color buckets and flowers. On escort cards, use a rubber stamp to print an image of a sand pail or a bouquet of flowers, and color code the picture in ink or paint to correspond to each guest's table.

pop-out table numbers

I'm always on the lookout for imaginative ways to make easy-to-read yet stylish table numbers. A children's pop-up book became the inspiration behind these numbered cards, cut from standard-sized sheets of basic card stock. With a bone folder, I scored each sheet down the center. The resulting fold served two purposes: It enabled each card to stand freely, and it became the center of each numeral. On scrap paper, I mapped out patterns for five-inch-tall numerals—simple lines and basic shapes work best—then sketched a number on the inside of each folded sheet. The idea is to cut out half of each numeral so the pop-out edges mirror the cutout on the card. Plan to waste a few sheets of paper in the process of drafting your cards.

8½ x 11-inch sheet of card-weight paper, 1 per table, plus extra sheets for practice

8½ x 11-inch sheet of 2 x 4-inch transparent laser printer labels, available at stationery stores; 1 sheet contains 10 labels

Ruler

Pencil

Bone folder

Straight-edge knife

Cutting board

Access to a computer and printer, unless hand-lettering the cards, in which case use calligraphy or fine-point markers

1. Fold each page of card stock in half vertically. Use the bone folder to smooth the crease.

2. On the inside fold of the card, pencil the shape of the table number. Use the ruler to draw any straight lines. Place the paper on the cutting board and use the straight-edge knife to cut along the edges of *half* the number only—do not cut past the crease line.

3. Using a desktop computer program, typeset the word "table." If you like, match the font to your menu or place cards. To save paper, copy the word five times, in two columns, on a single page, but leave several line spaces between each word. Many programs enable you to format the page according to the label size: See label package for specific instructions. Using a compatible printer, print out on clear sheets of laser labels in an ink color that complements your card stock.

4. On the cutting board, trim the labels as desired with the straight-edge knife, using the ruler as a guide. Crack and peel off the backing, then apply a label to each card in the corner underneath the cutout.

TABLE

TABLE

place card overlay

Paper overlays not only protect fabric tablecloths, they also introduce a novel—and clutter-reducing—place card option. For a country-style wedding, I set casual tables, using tumblers in lieu of stemware and river stones rather than napkin rings. And instead of place cards, I wrote guests' names right on the paper squares. Butcher paper has the perfect surface for lettering and other hand-painted embellishments. The unexpected flourish always charms guests.

Roll 48-inch-wide butcher paper, available from paper suppliers

Scissors

Yardstick

Black marker, to label pattern

Paint, or calligraphy or metallic markers

1. Cut four-foot lengths of butcher paper to make square overlays; one will cover a 36- or 48-inch round table. Or cut appropriate lengths for rectangular tables.

2. Make a pattern for the overlays. Place one paper square over a table the same size as the ones you'll be setting. Arrange plates and glassware on top of the paper square, and once you determine the best placement (a 48-inch round table can comfortably seat five or six people), use a black marker to boldly script names and decorative borders on the sample overlay. Names should be centered an inch above the edge of the dinner plate.

3. To detail the actual overlay, place the pattern underneath a fresh square of paper. The shadow of the script on the pattern will show through. Use it as a guide for lettering each overlay with paint, colored inks, or metallic markers and remove when completed.

Variations: Stamps or stencils make fast work of decorating paper. For a cake table overlay, use a smaller sheet of paper and script the entire surface with your monogram or words of inspiration.

place card napkin rings

One of the things you learn early in the event design business is that details count, and the proof is on the table. In my opinion, the most cohesive receptions feature smart tables set with clever accents. The key is to strike a balance between components that inject color and interest while remaining functional. Napkin rings that also act as place cards perform a dual service. Although, as is evident by the name, place cards are automatically assumed to be paper products, practically any smooth object that will hold lettering can indicate seating arrangements just as effectively. A lemon yellow acrylic square printed with green ink gives a modern edge to nubby silk napkins, and the citrus hues imbue the table with a fresh, summery zest.

Laser-cut acrylic squares, available at plastic suppliers and craft stores

Calligraphy or fine-point permanent markers

1. Use a marker in a color that complements your table décor to letter the acrylic squares with guests' names.
2. Thread a napkin through each ring and fluff the fabric for a fluid, shapely finish.

Variations: Look for other smooth objects with space for lettering to use as alternative place cards. Some readily available options include river stones, synthetic fruits like pomegranates, tiny terra-cotta pots, miniature porcelain pitchers, acrylic or glass boxes, and galvanized pails.

mark quinn

max kelly

kelly

champagne cage card holders

I love Champagne. Thank you, Dom Perignon, for this happy discovery! I can't imagine a wedding celebration without a bubbly toast. If you're fond of the effervescent brew, too, place card holders fashioned from wire cages make whimsical table accents. Collect cages from favorite vineyards, and save them from bottles shared on romantic evenings.

1 Champagne cage

Needle-nose pliers

1. Untwist the metal cage from the Champagne as you would if uncorking the bottle.
2. Use the pliers to make one cut through the band of wire that secured the cage to the bottle. Remove this band by sliding it out through the four tiny wire loops that will become the "feet" of the place card holder. Set aside.
3. Straighten the four "legs" of the cage and use the needle-nose point of the pliers to make sure the feet are twisted into well-turned coils. Insert the point of the pliers into the center of the tiny loops, then turn the tool slowly to adjust the tension of the coils.
4. Smooth out any kinks in the wire band that was clipped and removed in the first step. Then bend the band at its halfway point so that it resembles a large, wide hairpin. Use the needle-nose pliers to twist each end of this wire around the tops of two adjacent legs of the cage to create a "seat back."
5. Shape the seat back and correct the position of the legs so that the Champagne cage chair stands level on the tabletop. Because each cage is unique, expect each handcrafted chair to be slightly different.

acrylic tiles

When in doubt about the best way to enliven a table, think color. To plot my own experiments with color, I look to artists for inspiration. For a poolside celebration in Malibu, I skipped linens and instead dressed Saarinen tables with acrylic tiles, mixing primary colors and quadrilaterals à la Mondrian. Per my instructions, the plastic supplier engraved additional tiles with numbers, to be used to identify tables. Intrinsically reflective, the tiles perfectly complemented the acrylic chairs, a bar framed by glowing vases of blue water, and the hundreds of twinkling candles that floated on the surface of the pool.

4 2 x 4-inch yellow acrylic tiles

2 2 x 4-inch blue acrylic tiles

2 4 x 4-inch blue acrylic tiles

2 2 x 2-inch blue acrylic tiles

2 2 x 2-inch yellow acrylic tiles

1. From a plastic supplier, have tiles cut to order and engraved with table numbers.
2. As close to the event as possible, peel the protective paper from the tiles. Handle with care: Plastic is easily scratched.
3. Arrange tiles in an alternating pattern in the center of the table. Include one engraved tile per grid, to indicate the table number.

Variations: Suppliers can detail plastic in many ways and laser-cut the material into myriad forms. For example, numerically engraved frosted acrylic rectangles can be bent into L- or T-shaped easels for a three-dimensional presentation. Or have large individual squares of acrylic engraved in one corner with table numbers and use them as place mats for votive candles.

menu place cards

Guests love the welcome that personalized place cards deliver, and I love the way wonderfully lettered ephemera dresses up a table. Happily, one of the snappiest solutions to setting a table is also extremely easy on the wallet. Why? Whenever it's possible to combine more than one element of the celebration you're likely to save money. Menus that double as place cards eliminate the cost of an additional stationery item. Glassine sleeves are available in a variety of sizes and can be lettered with most inks. Simply insert a graphically composed menu to create a clever combination.

20-pound colored bond paper, 1 sheet per menu

4 x 6-inch sleeve-style glassine envelopes, 1 per menu

Ruler

Pencil

Paper cutter

Calligraphy marker

Gum eraser

Access to a computer and printer

1. Compose your menu. List items in order of service and include descriptive details for each course. Use a desktop computer program to graphically arrange the text into a square of type. For a contemporary design, alternate the size of the type for each course.

2. Format your page layout so that the menu text is centered to print on a standard sheet of bond paper. Print out the menus and trim to a uniform size—3¾ x 5½ inches—that will fit inside the glassine envelopes.

3. Prepare to letter the glassine envelopes with the guests' names. Orient the envelope so that the sealed bottom is at the top; the open end of the envelope will be the bottom. Use the ruler to pencil a very light guideline one inch from the top of the envelope.

4. Letter the glassine envelopes with a calligraphy marker in your favorite color. When dry, gently erase the guideline on each envelope. Insert menus into the sleeves.

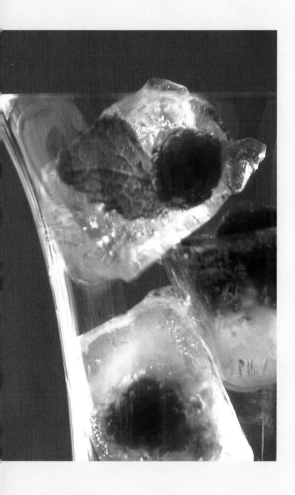

Because there are so many choices, the prospect of planning a reception may be daunting at first, but take a deep breath. How to serve your guests depends on what you serve your guests, when you want to serve them, and, of course, where. Once you decide on a date and location, you can begin to fill in the blanks. Let your caterer guide you through your options: Meals can be plated or served buffet- or family-style. Bars can be full-service or stocked with a limited selection of wine, beer, soda, and perhaps a signature cocktail. If you opt to serve several courses, consider starting with a seasonal soup. It looks elegant and is easy on the wallet. Keep buffets well-stocked, and never scrimp on wait staff. After determining your menu and service style, you can focus on the fun part—creating distinctive tabletop flourishes that will make the meal memorable.

cocktail stirrers

When the ceremony is over and it's time to celebrate, it's also time to sip a cocktail. On wedding days, everyone and everything are festively dressed. Why not decorate cocktails, too? Yes, there are commercially available stirrers, but I find they come in limited styles. When I design an event, I like to customize every single element. So when it comes to stirrers, if you want to turn heads while twirling ice cubes, it's best to make your own.

4-inch bamboo skewers, available at kitchen supply stores

Shells

Ribbons

Beads

Plastic pearls

Silk flower petals

Wired paper leaves

Quilling paper

Scissors

Metallic tape

Clear craft glue

24-gauge wire

Needle-nose pliers

To make seashell stirrers: Squirt a dime-sized dollop of glue on the inside of a shell. Insert the flat end of a skewer into the glue and hold until fixed in place. Let dry completely.

To make ribbon-flagged stirrers: Cut a three-inch strip of ribbon. Brush the inside with glue. Insert the flat end of a skewer at the midpoint of the ribbon, fold the fabric around the skewer, press flat, and let dry.

To make metallic-flagged stirrers: Cut a two-inch piece of metallic tape. Insert the flat end of a skewer at the midpoint of the tape, fold over and press tape ends together.

To make beaded stirrers: Thread beads or pearls onto a four-inch length of wire. Twist a tiny curl at each end of the wire with the pliers to secure the beads. Twist the beaded wire around a skewer tip.

To make leaved stirrers: Twist wired leaves around the flat end of a skewer.

To make silk flower stirrers: Dot the base of a silk petal with glue. Insert the flat end of a skewer into the glue and hold until fixed in place, then repeat, gluing on six additional petals in a circular pattern to create a flower. Glue a pearl in the center of the circle.

To make curlicue stirrers: Twist quilling paper into a tight circle, then let it relax. Dot the inside end of the paper with glue to attach to the skewer.

wine labels

One of the easiest ways to customize your reception is to create a wine label featuring your initials, wedding date, and even a pictorial motif designed to complement the décor. Although the vintage you pour will be traveling incognito if its label is covered, I still encourage couples to take the time to select a wine that not only tastes delicious but also holds some personal meaning. For a couple that met in, had family from, or felt connected to Italy in an important way, I'd suggest selecting a sparkling prosecco for the toast. Some vineyards also offer wines in colorful bottles that instantly brighten up tables.

Square of cover-weight (30-pound) paper, sized to fit over the bottle's original label

Paper discs with holes, available at office supply stores

Double-stick tape

20-inch length of gold-toned wire

6 celadon beads, available at craft stores

Assorted colorful markers or pens, available at art supply stores

Needle-nose pliers

1. Design a graphic motif for your labels. Initials, borders, or a sentimental notation like *a bella luna*, which translates as "beautiful moon," combine to create a charming label. Consider panoramic imagery, an illustration of the family home, or a repeating pattern of a decorative symbol such as a star. If the labels are to be hand-drawn, a simple design is easiest to replicate.

2. Design a graphic motif for the paper discs that echoes the design of the label, or simply letter the disc with the wedding date.

3. Use double-stick tape to adhere the label to the wine bottle. Place tape along the perimeter of the label's underside, then press in place.

4. Wind the gold wire around the neck of the bottle at least three times, threading it with two beads each time you circle the neck. Before twisting the ends of wire together, thread them through the hole in the paper disc. Twist the wire ends together once, then pull them wider apart and twist each one into a tiny coil.

Variations: Take any design—just be sure the artwork is dark enough to conceal the original label—and have it color-copied. Then cut the new labels to size and adhere over the preexisting labels with a glue stick.

assorted coasters

The most fashionable accessory for a signature cocktail is a customized coaster. Sure, you can buy ready-made doilies or printed paper discs, but I prefer to use unusual elements to personalize commercially available coasters or to craft coasters that are absolutely one of a kind. When coasters are this handsome I always suggest that they become a part of the table setting.

2 x 3-foot sheet of ⅛-inch-thick cork, available at hardware or craft stores

Fine-point pen

3-inch-round juice glass

Scissors

Gold spray paint

6 inches gold braid per coaster

Craft glue

5-inch silk squares sewn with a mitered hem

Adhesive crystals, available at craft stores

4-inch acrylic squares, available at plastic suppliers

Vinyl transfer type, available at art supply stores

Sheet graph paper

Pencil

Ruler

Tape

8½ x 11-inch-sheets of 80-pound cover stock

Hand embosser with initial, available to order at stationery shops

Gold ink rubber stamp pad

Small natural sponge

To make gold-coated cork coasters: Using the rim of the juice glass as a guide, trace three-inch circles with a pen onto the sheet of cork. The 2 x 3-foot sheet will fit at least 77 circles. Cut out the rounds with scissors. Cover your work surface with paper bags or newspaper and spray the rounds with gold paint. Glue a piece of gold braid to the rim of each coaster.

To make jeweled silk squares: Sew or purchase hemmed silk squares. Fold into a smaller square and press to set seams. Open flat and apply a crystal pattern to one corner of the square—the lilac napkin at left features a paisley design. Refold the napkin.

To personalize acrylic coasters that can double as place cards: Outline a four-inch square on the graph paper. Mark one guideline three-quarters of an inch below the top edge of the square. Tape an acrylic square to the graph paper, topside down. Use the guideline when transferring type to the underside of the coaster. To read properly when turned right side up, the letters need to be pressed in place in reverse order. Use a bone folder to rub lettering from the transfer paper to the acrylic. Remove the graph paper guide and reuse for the next coaster.

To make embossed squares: Cut cover stock into four-inch squares. Use the embosser to make an impression of the initial—or any customized design—in the center of each square. Ink a natural sponge on a rubber stamp pad and color the embossed initial with a few stamps of the sponge.

acrylic coasters

We all have our weak spots—for me, it's personalized coasters. I love heavy paper that's been letterpressed with patterns or initials; it's a wonderful way to add color, personality, and often a bit of whimsy to the celebration. Although the results are worthwhile, printing and embossing do take planning: You'll need to allow a few weeks for production. Whenever I have to create coasters on the quick, I start with acrylic discs, adhere favorite imagery to the underside, and trim to fit. As this assortment shows, virtually any design can be applied to the plastic.

Artwork: printed papers, color copies of old family photos, poetry, cartoon caricatures, decals

3-inch-round, ⅛-inch-thick acrylic discs, available from plastic suppliers

Paper cutter

X-Acto knife, available at art supply stores

Self-healing plastic cutting board

Kraft paper

Spray adhesive

Spray matte shellac

1. Select artwork for the coasters. Colorful papers are best. If working from a single original, replicate it using a color copier. With a paper cutter, trim the artwork into four-inch squares.

2. In a well-ventilated room, cover your work surface with kraft paper. Peel the protective backing off the acrylic discs and place them topside down. Lightly spray the backs with adhesive.

3. Place the artwork on the cutting board, visually center the disc above it, then put the sprayed side onto the paper, reposition as necessary, and press down to attach. Hold the disc in place with one hand, and with the other use the X-Acto knife to trim off the edges of the paper by cutting around the disc in one continuous motion. Set trimmed disc aside.

4. When all the discs have been trimmed, place them topside down on a fresh sheet of kraft paper and spray the paper backing with matte shellac to seal. Let dry. Add a second coat of shellac if necessary.

TO LOVE AND BE LOVED
IS TO FEEL THE SUN
FROM BOTH SIDES

—DAVID VISCOTT

iced teas

Summer weddings celebrated on balmy days depend on icy refreshments to keep guests content and cool. I suggest pouring tall drinks to quench thirsts. For a beach wedding, fruity collins-style mixes hit the spot. Champagne cocktails reflect the tone of more formal affairs. And at countrified receptions I like to serve spiked sun teas and fruity ades. For a vintage flourish, pour beverages from old glass milk bottles kept on ice in galvanized buckets or antique milk crates. Dress the bar in gingham cloths, and serve teas in tall tumblers filled with flavored ice cubes and garnished with sprigs of aromatic mint, with pitchers of honey and sugary syrup on the side for an even more charming presentation.

7 gallons water, preferably in plastic containers for easy use

20 tea bags each of Earl Grey, raspberry, and orange pekoe, to make 6 gallons tea

Sprigs of mint

Sprigs of chamomile

8 cups sugar

6 limes

3 lemons

3 oranges

2 pints raspberries

24 milk bottles

24 5-inch squares of cheesecloth

24 12-inch strands of raffia

Large pot

Wooden mixing spoon

Marker for labeling

3 place cards

1. Three days before the wedding, mix the sugar and one gallon of water in the large pot and simmer over low heat, stirring slowly, to make a simple syrup. Let cool, transfer to a container, cover, and store at room temperature until ready to use.
2. Two days before the wedding, make sun teas. Submerge 10 bags of the same flavor tea in a gallon container of water and let steep overnight or until infused. Discard tea bags.
3. The day before the wedding, clean the fruit and slice the citrus into wheels. Place one cup of each fruit into a different milk bottle, macerate slightly with the wooden spoon, then fill with the preferred tea. Add sprigs of mint or chamomile as desired.
4. Wrap a square of cheesecloth over the top of each bottle and knot in place with a raffia strand.
5. Letter place cards with the names of the iced teas, using one card to identify each flavor. Position the place card at the base of each bottle on the service bar.
6. To serve, fill glasses with ice cubes and pour in tea. Offer with pitchers of honey and the simple syrup so that guests can sweeten to taste.

cocktails

Perhaps the easiest way to personalize a wedding is to serve a signature cocktail. Shaken or stirred, a specialty drink instantly says "swank soirée." Of course, you may opt to stock a full bar, but I find that if you designate one drink in particular as the celebratory cocktail it makes more of a statement. Whatever potion you pour, top it with an eye-catching garnish: Star fruit, currant clusters, rose petals, and chocolate shavings all make a real sweet splash.

Cocktail shaker with strainer and swizzle stick

Ice

Stemware

Ingredients as listed in the individual recipes at right

To make a rosy martini: In a cocktail shaker, mix ice with equal amounts of cranberry juice and Pearl vodka plus a splash of triple sec. Pour through a strainer into stemware. Garnish with rose petals.

To make a sexy Champagne kir: Mix 2 tablespoons of frozen raspberry juice concentrate, 1 ounce raspberry liqueur, 1 ounce triple sec, and shake. Pour into a flute, top with Champagne, and garnish the glass with cluster of currants.

To make a cool blue cocktail: Shake together 2 ounces each of Bombay Sapphire gin and blue curaçao, ½ ounce each of lemon juice and Cointreau, and a splash of sour mix. Pour over a teaspoon of rock sugar. To make the pennant stirrer: Cut a 2 x ¾-inch paper flag, inscribe with a festive phrase, wrap the end around the tip of a swizzle stick and glue to adhere.

To make a decadent hot chocolate: Prepare hot chocolate mix according to package instructions, let cool, then shake with ice and 1 ounce each of milk and kahlua. Strain, pour into a glass, and garnish with a dollop of whipped cream and a sprinkling of chocolate shavings.

To make a tropical rum cocktail: Vigorously shake together ½ ounce lime juice, 1 ounce Midori, 1 ounce Bacardi rum, 3 ounces pineapple juice, and ice. Strain into a glass and garnish with a slice of star fruit.

To make a minty rum concoction: Mix 2 ounces Bacardi rum, ¼ ounce Cointreau, ½ egg white, 1 tablespoon lime juice, 1 tablespoon crushed mint leaves, and 1 teaspoon powdered sugar with ice. Shake vigorously until frothy. Strain into a flute, add several drops of crème de menthe, and garnish with a slice of lime.

Cheers to love

schnapps shots

The weather outside might be frightful, but a twilight winter wedding is delightful. Embrace winter receptions with a roaring hearth, and deck the halls, mantels, and tabletops with fragrant evergreen foliage and clusters of candles. To welcome guests in from the cold, offer them a bracing aperitif of peppermint schnapps, kept chilled in a bowl of fresh snow.

750 milliliter bottle peppermint schnapps; serves about 25

Box of white peppermint canes, 1 per shot, available at candy suppliers

Shot glasses, available to rent from party suppliers

Sprigs of silver leptospermum leaf to garnish the bowl

Bucket of fresh snow

5-inch-square brick of dry ice, available at ice vendors: see cautionary note in step 1

Cloth work gloves

Ice pick (optional)

Gallon-size zip-close freezer-style bag (optional)

15-inch silver punch bowl

1. The day before the wedding pick up the dry ice. Note: Do not touch the ice with bare hands. Ask the vendor to wrap the brick in heavy plastic. The wrapping will protect your hands from ice burns. Whenever handling the brick, wear cloth work gloves, not rubber or leather, which will stick to the ice. If necessary, use an ice pick to cut the brick down to a size that will fit in the punch bowl. Then place the piece in a gallon-sized zip-close plastic freezer bag and keep in a cooler until needed.

2. Place the wrapped brick in the punch bowl; cover and fill the bowl with snow. The dry ice will keep the snow cold and prevent it from melting.

3. Fill shot glasses with a short measure of schnapps—a little of this robust liquor goes a long way—then festoon each glass with a peppermint stick. Decorate the bowl with sprigs of leptospermum.

martini glass pyramid

Debonair cocktail parties glamorized on the silver screen in the 1940s defined celebratory style in a way that still feels modern. Renowned for smart repartee and swell appointments, films starring Fred and Ginger, Cary and Katharine, or Nick and Nora prove that urbane elegance is always in fashion. Martinis, the quintessential libation of the period, are once again all the rage. With a nod to these movie classics and their cocktail of choice, I often set bars with pyramids of glassware. To build these gleaming skyscrapers, use stemware with a broad base and cup—the shape provides the best balance. Flank the bar with two towers, or set one at the back like a sculpture.

**30 classic martini glasses,
available from party
rental suppliers**

1. Be sure your bar station is level. Determine what other items will rest on the bar and reserve a two-foot-square area of counter space for each glass pyramid. If covering the bar with table linens or decorating it with additional arrangements, set these in place first.
2. Within the designated space, arrange 16 martini glasses into a four-row grid. Be sure the glasses are as close together as possible.
3. Stand nine martini glasses on top of the first level by balancing each glass on the rims of the glasses below. Create a three-row grid.
4. Stand four martini glasses on top of the second level in the same manner, arranging them in a square.
5. Top the pyramid with a single glass.

Variations: For larger towers, layer each level with a ⅛-inch-thick square of acrylic cut to size. Use clear acrylic partitions for a modern look, transparent blue or chartreuse partitions to pick up the color palette of the celebration.

I've always been a fan of small weddings. A limited guest list allows the couple a wider range of location options, and the money they save across the board often affords them a few creative indulgences—like these feather-collared Champagne flutes. Dolled up glasses give a festive kick to table settings. And frankly, they're just so much fun to hold aloft while making a toast! It's easy to twist copper wire into action to attach feathers, beads, and other twinkling charms to the elegant stems.

6-inch strings of sewn feathers, 1 per flute, available by the yard at craft suppliers

2½ inches 22-gauge copper wire per flute

Needle-nose pliers

Champagne flutes

1. Prewash the flutes and let dry.
2. Wrap a string of feathers around the base of the flute's bowl and secure to the stem with a piece of copper wire. Twist the wire ends together with the pliers to fasten in place.

Variations: Use longer pieces of wire to gild the stems, or thread the ends with glass beads for a bit of sparkle. Sewn feathers, available in a variety of colors and styles, make fabulous ornamental collars for floral bouquets, glass hurricanes, and candle votives.

fruity ice cubes

I always suggest that couples serve a signature cocktail—it's an elegant way to personalize the wedding and stretch reception dollars. Mixing a tasty concoction is as simple as blending one part fruit juice with one part liquor or sparkling wine, but what makes any cocktail more glamorous are the finishing touches. One of the prettiest, and easiest to prepare, are fruity ice cubes. Slip a couple into any cocktail; guests will be pleasantly surprised.

Drinking water

Ice cube trays

Fresh raspberries

Fresh mint sprigs

Plastic tubs or freezer bags to hold finished cubes

1. Calculate your needs: Allow one cup of water for each standard-sized, 16-cube tray, and expect to use two or three cubes per cocktail.
2. Rinse the raspberries and mint sprigs, then separate the sprigs into individual leaves. Set both aside.
3. Partially fill trays with water—filtered tap water is fine, or use your favorite bottled brand. Drop one raspberry and one mint leaf into each cube slot, then place trays in the freezer.
4. When cubes are frozen solid, empty the trays into plastic tubs or freezer bags and immediately return the finished cubes to the freezer. If they melt just a tiny bit, they will stick together. Reuse the trays for the next batch. Fruity ice cubes can be made a week in advance.

Variations: With a melon ball utensil, scoop out orbs of watermelon, honeydew, and cantaloupe to freeze into cubes. Or freeze your favorite fruit juices—cranberry, grapefruit, lemonade—to make colorful, flavorful cubes that won't dilute cocktails as they melt.

gazpacho on ice

Sooner or later every reception boils down to one big question: How to feed the masses? Everybody knows that a hungry guest is a cranky guest, so when circulating hors d'oeuvres, the key is timing. Send out several trays as soon as guests arrive, and calculate five to six hors d'oeuvres per person—the caterer's rule of thumb. One of my favorite appetizers is a seasonal soup served like a cocktail. On summery days, spicy gazpachos hit the spot. They're easy to prepare in advance, they're filling, and they make a colorful presentation.

Your favorite yellow and green gazpacho

Radishes, julienned

Lime, cut into sidecar wedges

Sea salt flakes

Shallow bowl for salting glasses

15-inch-round galvanized tray

5-ounce juice glasses

Demitasse spoons

Cracked ice, available from ice suppliers

Large plastic juice pitchers

1. Prepare your favorite gazpacho recipes or other chilled soups two days in advance. Calculate a three-ounce serving per guest. Refrigerate the soups in large plastic juice pitchers. When ready to serve, simply shake and pour.

2. Julienne radishes the day before the wedding. Cover with a moist paper towel to keep fresh, and refrigerate overnight.

3. Have cracked ice delivered the day of the event. Store in a large cooler to keep handy. (You can also shatter ice by placing a tray's worth of cubes in a clean cotton cloth, gathering it into a pouch, and hammering it with a rolling pin or cleaver to crack.)

4. Reserve one glass for spoons, and presalt the rims of the rest the morning of the celebration: Rub a lime wedge around each rim, turn upside down, and dip in a shallow bowl of sea salt. Sticky citrus juice acts as a natural adhesive.

5. Pour soups into the salted glasses. Top each serving with a spoonful of radish confetti and garnish with a lime wedge.

6. Fill a galvanized tray with two inches of cracked ice. Place the demitasse spoons in the reserved juice glass and nestle it in the center of the tray. Surround with glasses of gazpacho.

Variations: In late autumn, pass wooden trays of bisque, chowder, or creamy risotto served in small mugs or porcelain teacups. And in the heart of winter, indulge guests with spicy hot toddies, cinnamon-garnished sips of steaming ciders, or thick cocoa topped with freshly whipped cream.

butter pyramids

Repackaging is a technique that caterers and event planners employ to ratchet up the style quotient of any celebration. It's an efficient use of resources: Buy large quantities of a basic item, then place it in a different, more decorative container, and tables or buffet stations are instantly dressed up at little expense. Take butter, for example, a staple at every dinner table: Rather than serve plain pats, I love to flavor butter with chopped herbs. Dotted with colorful flecks, butter pyramids look fancy, but are so easy to prepare. Whip up a batch weeks in advance and freeze until the day before the wedding. The savory spreads will add a gourmet accent to crusty breads and home-baked biscuits.

2 pounds butter

1 cup fresh rose petals, pesticide free

1 cup fresh tarragon

2 large mixing bowls

Chef's knife

2 spatulas

8 1-cup pyramid molds, available at kitchen supply stores

Plastic wrap

1. Bring butter to room temperature. Soften in one of the large mixing bowls with the spatula.
2. Keeping the two ingredients separate, rinse, then dry the rose petals and the tarragon. Chop finely. Set aside.
3. Using the second mixing bowl, divide the butter in half. With the spatula, fold the chopped rose petals into one pound of butter; fold the tarragon into the other pound of butter.
4. Line the molds with plastic wrap, then use the spatula to fill the molds with flavored butter. Press firmly to eliminate any air pockets. Cover with plastic wrap and place in a freezer.
5. When frozen, remove the butter from the molds. Rewrap the individual pyramids with plastic and return them to the freezer until the event. Allow a couple of hours to thaw butters at room temperature.

napkin bands

On a short list of the easiest ways to punctuate your table settings, napkin treatments compete for first place. Folded napkins bound with a bauble instantly decorate the table, and all it takes is a strip of vellum and a basic brass fastener to add buttoned-up polish to bundled utensils. On buffet tables, stack the tailored flatware in engraved silver platters.

8½ x 11-inch sheets of vellum in a color that complements the table settings

Paper cutter

Brass fasteners, available at office supply stores

20-inch-square napkins

Iron

Utensils

1. Use the paper cutter to trim vellum into 2 x 8-inch strips.
2. Fold napkins in half, then accordion-fold into 3 x 10-inch sections. Press with an iron.
3. Stack each napkin with utensils. Wrap one vellum band around the center of the napkin and utensils. Insert a brass fastener into the center of each band—the pointed tip of the fastener will puncture the vellum. Fold out the brass wings on the underside of the vellum band to secure.

Variations: Ribbons, tassels, braided cords, bands of printed paper, fabric cuffs secured with buttons, silk frogs, and beaded wires all make fancy closures.

napkin fold

In the most elegant establishments, tables will always be set with generous linens, because well-dressed ladies and gents need to protect their formal wear with ample napkin squares. To fit these supersized fabrics at individual place settings without overwhelming dinner plates, fold them into precise shapes that disguise their true breadth. Folded napkins can be used as neat tabletop sleeves for menus and place cards, and the combination of luxe linens and thick, textured papers makes for a regal presentation. An iron and a little practice are your best insurance for crisp folds.

24-inch-square linen napkin, available from linen suppliers

Iron

Booklet or flat page menu

Place card

1. Iron napkin.
2. Fold napkin in half horizontally.
3. Fold down the top layer to create a two-inch pocket. Then fold the remainder of this layer under itself to make a two-inch fold.
4. Pleat the bottom layer of the napkin to create a second one-inch pocket. Turn under the top edge to create a third pocket that is one inch deep.
5. Smooth fold lines, then visualize the napkin divided vertically into thirds. Fold the left and right thirds under themselves.
6. Lightly press again. Insert the menu into the bottom pocket fold. Center on the plate, and position the place card above it.

Variations: Fold linens into pyramids, or pleat into fans and tie one end with a ribbon, or roll into batons and belt with napkin bands. Ribbons come in so many luxurious fabrics, from plush velvets to tasseled braids to ethereal sheer organzas, that it's a cinch to transform even the plainest white napkin into a pretty table accent.

candles & votives

It may seem like an afterthought to many first-time celebration planners, but lighting is the easiest way to alter the personality of a room. Dim lights wrap guests in a warm, intimate cocoon, while brighter splashes of light add energy to dance floors and entrances. Most locations will offer at least basic electric lighting of some kind, which you can modify to match your scheme, and daytime receptions held in rooms with large windows may require less enhancement, though windowless venues obviously need help. But candlelight will always be my favorite way to dazzle guests. I love to cover tabletops, windowsills, and pathways with dancing flames. Candles couldn't be more affordable, they come in myriad sizes, colors, and styles, and their impact is unabashedly romantic. One good spark deserves another, so go ahead—stock up on wax, then grace your wedding day with a million points of light.

floating candles in tall vases

Tall glass vases filled with colored water and floating candles make dramatic centerpieces yet are simple to assemble and can be adapted in dozens of ways to suit your needs. Unlike ostentatious floral arrangements, transparent vessels expand sight lines—the water-filled vases act like picture windows. I love to use cylindrical vases to decorate food stations and bars. Their striking silhouette makes a statement that is both modern and romantic. Tint the water whatever color you like, and float a candle in a complementary hue.

3 24-inch-tall glass vases

2 20-inch-tall glass vases

10 gallons water

5 pink floating candles

Red food coloring

Stirrer

Butane torch

1. Line up the vases in a row. Alternate taller vases with shorter ones. Fill each with water to the same level.
2. Add about six drops of food coloring to one vase to tint the water. Stir to mix, and add more drops as necessary to intensify the color. When happy with the result, squeeze the same number of drops into each vase and stir to mix.
3. Float a candle in each vase. Light with the butane torch just before the reception.

Variations: Float candles in any water source: pools, fountains, birdbaths. Because candles will drift to the corners of the pools, double the quantity you plan to use—contrary to conventional wisdom, more is more when it comes to candles!

glass orb candlesticks

Want a reception for 200 to feel as intimate as one for 75? Add lots of candlelight. Since each flickering flame illuminates only the elements closest to it, the subtle glow makes any space cozier. When I'm using candles I love to set the tables with plenty of glassware. The clear, reflective surfaces maximize the impact of candlelight. To that end I created these glittering collars of glass orbs. They transform colored-glass candlesticks into ethereal columns of light.

8 glass orb ornaments of varying sizes per candlestick, available at holiday suppliers

8-inch length of 24-gauge wire per ornament

Wire cutters

Spool white florist tape

Glass candlesticks

1. Each glass orb is sold with a metal cap and loop meant to be used to hang the ornaments. Twist one end of a wire length securely around each ornament loop. Trim with wire cutters.

2. Wrap the metal cap and wire stem with a five-inch section of florist tape to cover and secure the wire to the ornament. Begin at the base of the cap, pull the tape to keep it smooth, and continue wrapping up just enough to conceal the twisted end of the wire length on the loop. Ideally, there will be no more than an inch of tape visible on each wire stem.

3. Fashion a mini garland out of eight wired and taped ornaments. I like to mix medium, small, even tiny orbs together. Start with a medium orb, place a small one next to it, and twist their wired stems together. Then line up another orb and twist it into place, varying the sizes and working in a linear direction to create a garland (as opposed to clustering the orbs into a bouquet shape).

4. When the mini garland is complete, trim any straggling stems, then simply loop it around the neck of the candlestick, twisting the end of the wire into the garland to secure the collar.

Variations: Glass ornaments come in a variety of colors. Use masses of orbs in your favorite shades to dress up your event. For a sparkling décor, large frosted silver ornaments make fabulous oversized wreaths or garlands.

grapevine candelabra

When I stumbled across a batch of wired faux grapevine in a silk flower shop I knew I'd found a treasure. Since that moment I've used the malleable vine to create all sorts of decorative embellishments. I like that I can quickly twist it into a shape, then unwind it just as easily if I change my mind. I wrap these vines around candelabra, pedestals, chandeliers, even stemware to add a touch of rustic vineyard chic to the celebration. Include ripe grapes as part of the centerpiece, then set the table with farm-fresh cheeses and flat breads, and guests will be enticed to start feasting as soon as they're seated.

4 stems 3-foot-long wired faux grapevine, available at silk flower suppliers

3-branch candelabra

Dinner plate that coordinates with the color palette

1 bunch each red and green grapes, well-washed

5 or 6 grape leaves: If fresh leaves are hard to find, faux leaves are available at silk flower suppliers

3 tapers

1. Twist the wired vine around each branch of the candelabra. Continue wrapping the entire candelabra, arranging the vine loosely for a natural appearance.
2. Set the wired candelabra on the decorative dinner plate.
3. Break each bunch of grapes into smaller clusters. Arrange around the base of the candelabra. Detail with grape leaves.
4. Insert tapers. If desired, use a bobeche or glass collar at the base of each candle to catch wax drippings.

One dramatically dressed candle can stand in for a dozen plain ones, especially when skirted with a pile of luminous bridal pearls. I love to accent tables with big, thick pillars in pretty colors set atop silver pedestals. They're a simple, appealing way to add some classic glamour to the reception. I also suggest couples consider including a single, decorated unity candle as part of their ceremony, and that they light it together after reciting their vows.

6 x 3-inch pillar candle

4-inch-round paper doily, available at bakery or party suppliers

4-inch-round silver pedestal, available at gift shops or flea markets

1 cup plastic pearls, available at craft stores

Glue gun

1. Heat the glue gun at your workstation, then use a small drop of hot glue to anchor the candle to the center of the doily.

2. Place the candle with the doily on the pedestal. With the glue gun, draw a thin strip of hot glue about two inches long around the base of the candle and dot with pearls. Continue working in two-inch segments so that the glue stays warm throughout the pearl application process. If the glue cools, simply draw another strip over the dried one.

3. Continue gluing rings of pearls around the candle base to create an inch-wide platform of pearls. Once this perimeter ring is complete, begin stacking the pearls up the pillar, using dots of glue to anchor each pearl in place. The goal is to create a multilayered skirt of pearls that climbs almost to the halfway point of the pillar.

Variations: Glittery beach stones or opalescent seashells, metallic glass ornaments, and even pinecones or small gourds make delightful candle collars.

garden lanterns

My mother spent the summer before my wedding crafting a hundred lanterns to stake across the garden. On the day of the ceremony, colorful cellophane lanterns dotted our lawn, and they glowed throughout the evening. I followed mom's blueprint to create lantern bases from wood dowels and sheets of celadon cellophane. Also known as photo gels, this material is used as a filter by professional photographers and is available at photo supply stores.

5-foot-long, 1-inch-round dowel

4-inch-square of ½-inch-thick wood

4 8-inch-long, ½-inch-square dowels

4 3-inch-long, ½-inch-square dowels

Saw (optional)

Can green spray paint

Drop cloth or cardboard box, to cover work surface when spray-painting

5 1-inch nail brads

Hammer

Wood glue

8 x 16-inch sheet of diffusion paper, available at professional photography equipment suppliers

8 x 16-inch sheet of transparent celadon cellophane, also known as photo gels, available at professional photography equipment suppliers

Staple gun

6-inch-tall glass votive

3-inch-tall pillar candle

Florist clay

Butane torch

1. Buy wood cut to order from a lumber supplier, or use a saw to cut your own. In a well-ventilated area, spray all the wood cuts with green paint to cover. Protect your work space with a drop cloth or use a long cardboard box as a shield to absorb any excess paint.

2. Assemble the box frame. Use the four-inch square for the base. Nail an eight-inch-long square dowel to each corner of the base with a brad. The nail should pass through the bottom of the base up into the center of the dowel. Complete the frame by placing a three-inch dowel horizontally between each pair of vertical posts and adhering with wood glue.

3. Attach the long, round dowel to the base of the box frame with wood glue. Then hammer a nail through the top of the square base down into the center of the long dowel to secure.

4. Layer the diffusion paper over the cellophane; then, with the diffusion paper facing out, use the staple gun to anchor one eight-inch side of both sheets to one of the corner dowel posts of the box frame. Wrap the papers around the box, attaching with additional staples. Up to this point, lanterns can be made weeks in advance of the event.

5. The day of the event, place a quarter-sized wad of florist clay on the underside of the votive glass and press it into the base of the lantern box to adhere. Insert the candle in the votive, and light with the butane torch.

bamboo torch

Balmy breezes, lullaby waves, a blanket of soft sand, and a vast blue sky that melts into an infinite ocean: It's no wonder so many couples dream of exchanging vows on the beach. Nature's paradise needs little adornment, but bamboo accents blend right into the scenery while still serving a practical function. Fringed with palmetto fronds and topped with votive candles, an aisle of bamboo torches turns any beach into a tropical oasis.

5-foot-long, 4-inch-wide pole of green bamboo, available at specialty garden supply centers

5 stems palmetto foliage

Skein natural raffia

Round glass votive with candle

¼-cup sand

¼-cup beach pebbles

2-gallon galvanized bucket

1 quart bag quick-dry concrete, available at hardware stores

6-foot-long, 3½-inch-wide length of PVC pipe

Craft glue

Shovel (optional)

Butane torch

1. Create a weighted base to anchor the bamboo securely in place in case of high winds or an awkward guest. With the galvanized bucket and the PVC pipe on hand, prepare the concrete. Immediately pour it into the bucket and stand the PVC pipe upright in the center of the mix. If it isn't already, fill the pipe with two inches of concrete. Hold the pipe in position as the concrete hardens. Let dry completely. This step can be done weeks in advance of the wedding.

2. Use craft glue to attach the votive to the top of the bamboo pole.

3. The day before the wedding, use raffia to wrap palmetto leaves around the top of the pole a few inches beneath the votive. Store carefully.

4. Carry the bucket and the bamboo pole to the beach. Place the bucket at the spot you want to locate the torch, then fill it with sand to further weigh it down. For added stability, dig a hole in the sand and bury the bucket just below the surface.

5. Fill the votive with the quarter-cup of sand and the quarter-cup of beach pebbles, then insert the candle. Keep craft glue handy, in case the votive comes loose and needs to be reattached. Thread the bamboo on top of the PVC pipe. Light the candle with the butane torch.

gold mesh lantern

I love to travel, and every new city beats with a culturally distinct pulse that never fails to inspire me. Large cities tend to be magnets for arts from distant ports, so finding paper lanterns from Morocco on a trip to Prague made perfect sense. These exotic luminaries were simple structures—square panels of waxed paper lettered with arabesque calligraphy and laced with linen thread. I decided to reinterpret the lamps in modern-day gold mesh, and this basic shape is easy to re-create in any fabrication.

½-yard gold metal mesh cut into 4 5-inch squares

4 15-inch lengths of ¼-inch gold metal mesh ribbon

16 4 x ½-inch strips of heavyweight chipboard

7-foot length of wired cord

Screw punch, also known as a Japanese push drill

Scissors

Bone folder

Glass votive with candle

1. Lay the chipboard strips into four-inch-square shapes centered on top of each mesh square. A one-inch perimeter of mesh should surround each chipboard square. Fold this perimeter over the chipboard to make four-inch-square mesh panels. Use the bone folder to smooth hems. The mesh needs no adhesive: Its hundreds of tiny wires will hold the chipboard in place.

2. Use the screw punch to make a row of five holes along the parallel sides of each panel—one in each corner, three equally spaced between the top and bottom holes. Punch the holes through the two mesh layers and the chipboard between them.

3. Lace two panels together with one length of mesh ribbon. Fold the ribbon length in half to determine its center point, then lace from the top down. Cross as if lacing a pair of sneakers. Repeat until the four panels are laced into a cube. Tie the ribbon ends with square knots and fray for a decorative finish.

4. Cut two two-foot lengths of wired cord from the seven-foot length. Fold the pair of cords in half and twist a one-inch circle from the top. This loop will be used to hang the lantern. Attach an end of cord to each inside corner of the cube by twisting it around the laced mesh ribbon.

5. Cut two 10-inch lengths from the remaining cord and twist together at the five-inch mark. Center the votive between the four cords and twist the ends together underneath the glass to secure. Use the last length of cord to suspend the votive by wrapping one end around the twisted cords above the votive and the other around the base of the lantern's loop. Adjust the length as necessary so the votive hangs in the middle of the lantern.

grapevine votive

Gardens planted with candles create an enchanted into-the-woods mood. I especially love the way trees turn into organic sculptures when I hang votives from their limbs. Clusters of candles draw guests like moths to flames, and candle-filled trees can be used to designate the perimeters of an outdoor reception space. Flickering arbors are most effective when the votives are liberally strung. If you ask me, there's no such thing as too many candles.

Spool nylon monofilament

Scissors

1-inch-round metal ring washer (optional)

3-foot length of wired faux grapevine

Glass votive with 12-hour candle

Butane torch

1. Use nylon filament to create a sling to hang the votive. If the votive does not have a lip, cut three 12-inch strands of nylon filament and knot one end of each strand to the washer. Center the washer under the votive. Pull the three strands up and around the votive and knot the ends together. If the votive has a lip, encircle the votive under the lip with nylon filament, then tie three bracing connections of filament to the circle and knot them together. Tie a single strand of nylon filament around the knot of three ends. Tie this single strand to the tree branch at the desired length.
2. Place the candle into the hanging votive.
3. Wrap the length of grapevine around the votive. Twist the tail end into a spiral, and the top end up around the nylon filament.
4. At dusk, light the candle with the butane torch.

cylinder wraps

Glass cylinders are versatile containers. They hold flowers and make ideal hurricanes for candles. I buy glass vases in caseloads, since they're always cheaper by the dozen, then experiment with every imaginable decoration: vellum, raffia mesh, even flower blossoms. I'm always excited to discover what new material will magically diffuse candlelight.

4 9 x 3-inch glass cylinders

4 3-inch votive candles

4 stems lime green chrysanthemum: yields about 30 blooms

Clippers

Glue gun

9 x 13-inch sheet of raffia mesh

30-inch length of thin silk cord

Metal rosette button, available at bead shops

Craft glue

9 x 12-inch sheet of printed vellum

Screw punch, also known as a Japanese push drill

2 7-inch lengths of thin satin ribbon

Scissors

Spray adhesive

9 x 12-inch sheet of marbled vinyl

Paper cutter

Ruler

Pencil

Grommet kit containing ⅛-inch grommet tool and 10 grommet rings, available at hardware stores

30-inch length copper-colored ribbon

To make a floral-studded cylinder: Trim the blooms off the stems to get flat button chrysanthemum heads. Use the glue gun to attach the flowers to the glass. Begin with dense coverage at the base of the cylinder and disperse the flowers up the sides of the glass toward the rim. Make the day before the wedding and keep cool until use.

To make a mesh-wrapped cylinder: Wrap the sheet of raffia mesh around the cylinder and use tiny dabs of craft glue to secure. Belt the thin silk cord three times around the center of the glass, knot, and use a dab of craft glue to anchor the metal rosette button in place.

To make a vellum-veiled cylinder: Use the screw punch to punch out a pattern in the sheet of printed vellum—I selected a daisy design, and punched out the centers of about one fourth of the flowers. Spray the reverse side of the vellum with adhesive, then wrap the sheet around the cylinder to attach. Trim at the top and bottom with a length of thin satin ribbon, allowing at least a one-inch overlap of ribbon. Adhere with craft glue and snip ribbon ends with sharp scissors for a clean finish.

To make a corset-style cylinder: Wrap the marbled vinyl around the cylinder to estimate, then trim with the paper cutter to allow for a quarter-inch vertical gap between the two ends. With the ruler and the pencil, measure and lightly mark positions for five pairs of holes, equally spaced, set about a quarter-inch in from the vertical edges of the vinyl. The top and bottom pairs of holes should rest about a half-inch in from the horizontal edges of the vinyl. Follow the directions on the kit to punch grommet holes in the vinyl. Lace the copper ribbon through the holes and tie it in a bow at the top.

Candlelight makes any celebration sparkle. I always suggest couples spend money on candles—the magical impact created by a fleet of twinkling tea lights certainly offers the best bang for each reception buck. Long-burning votive candles are a party planner's best friend. Buy them by the gross and scatter them everywhere. For a seaside wedding I used basic glass tumblers as hurricanes. The glasses I chose were well-weighted at the base, and slightly broader than the standard votive. This extra space allowed me to design miniature beachscapes of white sand and bleached seashells, and I completed the charming tableaux with candles as azure as a summer sky.

Small seashells, available on beach walks or at nautical gift shops, 1 handful per candle

Glass tumblers, 1 per candle, available by the case at kitchen supply stores

¼ cup sand or ¼ cup pebbles per candle, available at pet stores specializing in tropical fish

2-inch-tall 8-hour votive candles in a color that complements the palette and will stand out against the sand

1. If you've scavenged beach shells, it's necessary to clean them. Soak them with a cup of chlorinated bleach diluted in a bucket of tap water. Rinse well, then let dry in the sun to further bleach away the briny smell. Brush off any remaining seaweed debris.
2. Remove any labels from the tumblers. Fill each with a quarter cup of sand or pebbles.
3. Nestle a candle in the sand or pebbles. Scatter seashells around each candle's base.

Variations: Create candlelight tableaux with large rectangular vases that can hold several candles. For a more formal affair cluster together mismatched wine glasses and fill with sand, seashells, and candles.

silvered luminaries

Metallic accents make receptions glitter, and candlelight has a special affinity for shiny finishes, bouncing from one reflective surface to another. One affordable way to create a dazzling spectacle of dancing flames is to adhere sheets of silver leaf to basic glass vases. The leaf will naturally flake off in places, allowing the light from the candle within to flicker through the cracks.

2 2½ x 3½ x 8-inch glass vases

5 glass votives

12-inch square of Mylar with adhesive backing

12 4-inch squares of silver leaf

Spray adhesive

Spray matte shellac

Star stencil

Pencil

Scissors

Natural bristle paintbrush

Disposable work gloves

Newspaper or paper bags to cover work surface

1. Work in a well-ventilated room, and cover your work surface with newspaper or old paper bags. Don work gloves. Spray the outside of the vases and votives with a coat of adhesive.
2. On the back of the Mylar square, stencil stars in various sizes. Cut out with scissors. Plot your placement beforehand, then peel off the adhesive backing and stick stars to the sides of the vases. Opt to wrap at least one star around a corner of each vase.
3. Silver leaf comes in extremely thin sheets. Use the paintbrush to lift each sheet from its protective packaging. Smooth the silver leaf in place on top of the tacky surface of the vases and votives with your fingertips and the paintbrush. Rub gently to finish. The silver leaf will tear a bit, and that's good—it gives the vases a crackled, antiqued appearance.
4. Spray a coat of matte shellac to seal the silver leaf and the Mylar stars to the vases and votives.

lavender luminary

Freshly harvested lavender emits an evocative fragrance that reminds me of lazy summer days. When laced with a collar of these aromatic herbs, basic glass vases become fanciful hurricanes. Lavender spires bloom in a range of colors, from pale silver to deep purple, so visit the nearest farmers' market to see what varieties are available in your area. Dried herbs resist the wilting heat of a candle, but be sure to use a short pillar inside a tall glass hurricane to keep the flame well away from the floral wrapping.

7 bunches lavender, 30 stems each

Clippers

12 x 4-inch cylindrical glass vase

Spool green florist tape

Skein raffia

6 x 3-inch pillar candle

Butane torch

1. Trim the lavender stems with the clippers. Individual stems should vary in height, but all should have a common flat edge.
2. Start to encircle the vase with lavender, securing the stems to the glass with florist tape. The stems should lie flat against the glass. Pack them close together for dense coverage. Continue taping stems until the entire circumference of the vase is covered.
3. Wind raffia over the florist tape to conceal. Expect to wrap around the vase about 25 times to create a band of raffia that's approximately one inch wide. Cut and knot the ends together.
4. Place the candle in the vase and light with the butane torch just before the reception begins.

Variations: Use lavender ribbon to conceal the florist tape. For a minimalist version, gather a handful of lavender stems into a small bundle and tie with raffia. String celadon beads on the ends of the straw. Use more raffia or a lavender ribbon to tie the small bundle to the vase.

wedding cake tables

It's more than sugar and butter that makes wedding cakes so delicious to behold. The secret ingredient is a heaping cup of good old-fashioned sentiment. Personalize your cake table with passionate red petals, a glistening pedestal of pearls, or three tiers of cupcakes, and guests will be touched by the sweetness of your gesture. The tradition of cutting the cake symbolizes hope and commitment, and it seems to me that as our regard for these aspirations has grown, so, too, have wedding cakes evolved to ever more fanciful heights. Happily, there are many talented bakers just waiting to whip up the cake of your dreams. Once you decide on the flavor and decorative style—a seriously tasty responsibility—leave the baking to the pros and devote your time to dressing the table. Look for plates and linens to complement the pretty confection: Chances are, second to you, it will be the most photographed beauty of the day.

three tiers of cupcakes

Couples who prefer to host a fun, slightly less formal celebration may want to consider this charming alternative to the classic three-tiered wedding cake. The stacked glass plates playfully mimic the lines of traditional tiers, and the individual portions make it easy for guests to serve themselves. Plus, there's something irresistible about cupcakes. With their shiny foil wrappings, thickly iced tops, and sugar blossom bows, each one is like a little edible present.

18-inch-round paper doily, available at bakery or party suppliers

18-inch-round, ¼-inch-thick glass plate

12-inch-round glass pedestal

6-inch-round glass pedestal

Calligraphy marker

Cupcakes

1. Use the calligraphy marker to script the couple's names around the perimeter of the doily.
2. Center the 18-inch round of glass on the cake table— ideally a 30-inch round table draped with white linen.
3. Top the glass round with the scripted doily.
4. Center the 12-inch pedestal on the doily. Top with the 6-inch pedestal.
5. Fill the three tiers with cupcakes.

Variations: For couples with large guest lists, custom cuts of glass can accommodate more cupcakes. Separate tiers with silver candlesticks hot-glued between the glass plates. Decorate each tier with a scripted paper doily, or sandblast or etch glass with the couple's names, the wedding date, or an ornate border. The engraved platters will become cherished keepsakes.

acrylic cake stand

Transparent sheets of plastic have added a new dimension to wedding receptions. I'm always thinking of inventive ways to play around with this versatile material, because I love how light travels through it. Boxy shapes are the easiest to craft from acrylic panels. To make a luminous plinth for a wedding cake, I stacked graduating trays under the ribbon-striped confection.

2 16-inch-square, ¼-inch-thick acrylic panels, for the top and bottom

4 2 x 16-inch, ¼-inch-thick acrylic panels, for the sides

2 14-inch-square, ¼-inch-thick acrylic panels, for the top and bottom

4 2 x 14-inch, ¼-inch-thick acrylic panels, for the sides

Acrylic solvent and application syringe

1. Have acrylic panels cut to order by a plastic supplier.
2. At your workstation, separate the panels into two groups—one for the 16-inch-square box, the other for the 14-inch square. Peel the protective paper from the acrylic panels. The plastic scratches easily, so handle with care.
3. Use acrylic solvent to adhere the first group of panels into a 16-inch-square box. Draw a thin bead of adhesive down the ¼-inch width of the two-inch edge of one of the side panels, glue it at a right angle to another side panel, and hold in place until bonded. Repeat with the other side panels to complete the square frame. Draw a thin bead of the adhesive all along the ¼-inch perimeter and top with one of the 16-inch squares. When dry, flip over and repeat to complete the 16-inch-square box.
4. Repeat the previous step with the second group of panels to make the 14-inch-square box.
5. Stack the smaller box on top of the larger one to create a tiered base for a cake.

Variations: For real drama and a more majestic base, stack three graduated acrylic boxes to the same height as the real cake. To mirror the cake, each acrylic tier should be two inches smaller in diameter than the one below it. Add color and interest by filling the acrylic boxes with colorful petals, pearls, confetti, or crystals before sealing closed.

heirloom cake cloth

Both majestic and sweet to behold, a wedding cake is a star attraction of any reception. At every celebration I attend, I delight in the throngs of children, many on tiptoe, pressing for a closer peek at the delightful confection. Youngsters like these represent a hopeful future, while our ancestors symbolize the generational ties that anchor us. Couples can commemorate such bonds by displaying old family photos of previous newlyweds. Apply photo transfers to a smooth fabric like silk or linen, and the charming mementos make an engaging, imaginative table cover—as well as a sensational keepsake long after the celebration has ended.

Black-and-white family photos

Ink-jet printer

8 sheets ink-jet-compatible transfer film, available at art and office supply stores

Ruler

Pencil

Scissors

Cellophane tape

30-inch-square tablecloth, preferably in white silk or linen

Iron, preheated to cotton setting

Linen ironing cloth

1. Collect favorite photos and scan them.
2. I prefer snapshots that are uniform in size. If the proportions of your portraits vary greatly, which is likely when choosing photographs from different decades, you can make adjustments on your home computer. Computer programs also allow you to retouch and otherwise customize the images.
3. Print out multiple copies of the images from your home computer on transfer film made specifically for ink-jet printers. (Beware: These sheets are not compatible with heat-generating laser printers.) Each sheet of transfer film can accommodate six 2 x 3-inch images. For the cloth pictured, I began with nine family photos and made five copies of each—just enough to create a collage that fully decorated the fabric.
4. Cut out the images from the transfer film, leaving a ⅛-inch margin around each print. Then place the prints on the cloth to determine the ideal pattern. Arrange them so that duplicate images are not adjacent to each other. Temporarily tack each photo in place with a bit of tape.
5. Transfer the images to the fabric using a dry, hot iron. If you haven't already, turn the image so that it faces the fabric. Then cover the back with a linen ironing cloth and heat evenly for several minutes. Check the fabric. When the transfer is complete, the paper backing will peel away easily. Repeat for each print.

Variations: Most copy centers produce transfers and adhesions as a basic service. This timesaving option still requires your creative direction about the placement of the photographs.

pearl cake pedestal

I love to present smaller wedding cakes on pedestals. Happily, it's not hard to transform plain plates into totally unique platforms. I find that pearls, the opalescent orbs so often used to bejewel the necklines of bridal gowns, are equally flattering for wedding cakes.

10-inch-round pedestal

8 30-inch strands of ⅜-inch-round plastic pearls

Glue gun

Scissors

Small bowl

Long-handled tweezers, available at craft and bead stores

1. The easiest way to accomplish the beading is to work with linear strands of pearls. Since they are typically sold as necklaces, you'll have to cut the string to get straight segments. Find the knot in the necklace, then cut the string below it. The knot will keep pearls from sliding off one end; pinch the other end for the same purpose. Remove about five pearls from the open end of the string and set aside in the small bowl. Then knot the open end so that the remaining pearls are tightly strung. Prepare all the strands in this manner.

2. Flip over the pedestal. Squirt a large dot of hot glue where you want the first pearl to be placed on the plate's perimeter. Position the pearl so that the knot is submerged in the glue. Use the tweezers to hold the pearl in place while the glue cools. Draw a thin bead of glue and continue to attach the remainder of the strand about six inches of pearls at a time, pushing the beads gently into the warm glue with the tweezers. Work in a circular pattern from the outside in to create a seamless spiral of pearls across the bottom of the plate, then continue to glue pearls around the stem and the base of the pedestal. With each new strand, anchor the first and last pearl so that the knots are concealed by the glue.

3. Turn the plate right side up and inspect it for bare spots, loose beads, and threads of glue. Gently manicure with the tweezer, pulling off any excess glue bits and adding on individual pearls as needed to fill gaps.

4. Dot the outer edge of the plate with any remaining loose pearls.

Variations: Armed with a glue gun, it's easy to adorn almost any surface. Dot additional pearls directly onto the cloth skirt to add detail to the cake table. Also trim cake plates with beads of all sorts, shells, feathers, sequins, even silk petals.

petals under glass

Flowers are favored embellishments for wedding cakes. Their sensual shapes make a suitable garnish, although personally I prefer to use sugary, edible blossoms and save fresh petals to press under the glass top of a cake table. Hearty, affordable, and available in many shades, carnations are an excellent flower for this purpose. It's easy to coordinate the petals with the color of your icing. Simply snip petals from flower heads to create a fresh confetti.

2 bunches carnations; yields about 48 blooms

Scissors

30-inch-round, ¼-inch-thick glass tabletop

30-inch-round folding table

90-inch-round tablecloth

Plastic tub

1. Use scissors to cut the petals from the carnation heads. This technique is faster and neater than pulling off the petals one at a time from their base. Petals can be cut the day before the wedding. Store in the plastic tub and refrigerate.
2. Just before the reception, set up the folding table and cover with the cloth. Scatter the petals in a lush layer over the cloth, then top with the glass round.

Variations: Use more than one color of petals for a fanciful mosaic. Or create a collage of memorabilia and photographs that highlight moments from the day you met right up until the wedding.

floral swag

Draping tables or chair backs, doorways or columns with yards of silken fabrics sets a luxurious mood. Crisp taffetas, nubby silks, and polished cottons always deliver a theatrical punch, and whenever I add fresh flower tiebacks, the scene becomes a tour de force. Oasis domes are versatile tools for fashioning such floral accents. The real trick is securing the dome to its intended position; common household zip ties get the job done. Available at hardware stores, these thin strips of corrugated plastic have a small opening at one end: When the hole is threaded with the opposite, pointed end, then pulled tight, the tie forms a firm lock. To remove, simply cut the strip with clippers.

3-inch Oasis dome,
available at floral suppliers

Plastic tub

Clippers

9 stems lilac

4 stems vibernum

Large rose

Zip tie

1. Fill the plastic tub with water and immerse the Oasis dome. Remove when saturated, about 20 minutes.
2. Trim each stem with a diagonal cut before inserting it into the Oasis. Insert lilac blossoms first, in a circular pattern. Insert the rose toward the top of the dome. Add the vibernum randomly, to fill out the design. Make the arrangement no more than two days in advance, and keep refrigerated.
3. When ready to hang, thread the zip tie through the latticework cage on the back of the dome, then belt it around gathered fabric. Thread the tail into the opening and pull tight to secure. Fluff out the fabric beneath the flowers to finish the look.

Variations: One version of Oasis domes is sold with a suction cup attachment so that it can be anchored to almost any surface, from wooden pews to glass windows.

wedding cake canopy

Delightfully iced pastel tiers of pastry call for a theatrical setting. It makes sense to frame the cake in such a breathtaking manner—after all, it will be a major attraction, and the focus of many photographs. As dramatic as this canopy looks, it's actually quite easy to construct. A ring of mosquito netting hung from the limb of a shade tree becomes the perfect shelter. Embellish it with yards of blushing pink ribbon to craft what I fondly call a cake shrine.

84 yards of 3-inch-wide pink satin ribbon

Tape measure

Scissors

3-inch acrylic ring

8-foot-long mosquito net hung from a 24 or 28-inch ring, available at camping suppliers

Grommet kit containing ⅜-inch grommet tool and 5 grommet rings

3-inch snap clamp, available at hardware stores

½-inch-thick cable calculated to the length needed to suspend the canopy

Cable clamp, available at hardware stores

5 3-inch tent stakes, available at camping suppliers

10 feet of ⅛-inch braided white nylon cord

Hammer

30-inch-round folding table

90-inch-round pink underskirt

90-inch-round lace overlay

1. Cut the ribbon into 10-foot lengths, reserving one two-foot length. Knot one end of each ribbon to the acrylic ring, leaving a three-inch tail above each knot. When done, the ring will be concealed by ribbons.

2. Follow the kit instructions to punch five grommet holes, equally spaced, around the hem of the mosquito netting.

3. Slip the acrylic ring with the ribbons over the suspension cord attached to the mosquito netting. Wrap the two-foot length of ribbon around the acrylic ring to hide the knots. Connect the snap clamp to the mosquito netting's cord, then roll up the ribbons with the netting and store in a clean plastic bag until the morning of the event.

4. Determine the best place to hang the canopy. Allow for a clearance of seven feet and a perimeter of about eight feet. Loop the length of cable over a tree limb or trellis frame and temporarily anchor it in place with the cable clamp. Attach the opposite end of the cable to the snap clamp at the top of the netting. Adjust the length of the cable to suit the setting, then permanently clamp in place.

5. Set up the folding table directly under the canopy. Plot the position of the tent stakes—the hem should gently flare open to display the cake and accommodate guests—then use the hammer to drive them into the ground. Tie the netting to the stakes with nylon cord threaded through the grommets. Allow about two feet of cord per connection.

6. Just before the reception, cover the table with the pink underskirt, then top with the lace overlay. Center the cake beneath the netting.

wedding cake centerpiece

When asked for ideas on how to save money without sacrificing style, I always suggest looking for ways to get double duty out of decorative elements. For example, I love using small wedding cakes as centerpieces. In lieu of blooms, dress tables with mini cakes placed on pedestals. Studded with sugar leaves and flowers, their dressy attire makes a festive statement. When it's time to cut the cake, have one happily married couple at each table follow your lead and slice their sweet centerpiece in your honor.

12-inch-round silver pedestal

12-inch-round paper doily

10-inch basic buttercream cake per table of 10 guests

Box of premade mini sugar leaves

Box of premade large sugar leaves

Large premade sugar rose

1. Place the paper doily on the pedestal. Top it with the cake.
2. Decorate the sides of the cake with mini sugar leaves.
3. Top the cake with a large sugar rose. Ring it with large sugar leaves.

Variations: Basic bakery cakes or cupcakes can be ordered on short notice, and many types of edible ornaments are available from confectionery suppliers. Instead of roses, each cake could feature a candy version of your monogram. Set tables with cakes that are all decorated in the same manner, or ice each cake in a different rainbow color, or detail each one with different flowers or dragées.

sugar rose cake topper

Determining the appropriate cake topper is one of the trickiest decisions to make. Not only should it be in harmony with the design of the cake, it's also meant to be a keepsake. For this reason it's especially meaningful to create the topper yourself. For an easy embellishment that can be personalized in a hundred different ways, fill a handsome monogrammed silver cup with a cluster of porcelain-like sugar roses couched on gauzy layers of organza ribbon.

4 2-inch white sugar roses made from royal icing, available from confectionery suppliers

4 1-inch white sugar roses made from royal icing

Fine-point awl

2 cups white royal icing

Pastry bag with small tip

12 6-inch-long white paper sticks (used for lollipops), available from confectionery suppliers

2 yards white organza ribbon

Scissors

Spool thin white florist wire

2-inch metal frog

2 x 2 x 4-inch brick Oasis foam

Florist knife

5-inch-tall mint julep cup

1. Royal icing flowers are typically sold with a tiny hole in the back. Use the awl to create or deepen each small hole into a shallow pit that will accommodate the end of a paper stick.
2. Spoon royal icing into the pastry bag, then use dots of it to glue a stick in place at the back of each sugar rose. Let dry.
3. Cut the ribbon into four equal lengths. Loop each length back and forth to create a bow, tie at the center with a small piece of florist wire, and use a few more inches of florist wire to twist each bow to a paper stick.
4. Insert the frog into the narrow end of the Oasis brick. If necessary, trim the foam with the florist knife to fit, then place the brick in the cup. Insert the paper sticks securely into the foam to arrange the sugar roses, then add the wired bows.

Variations: Use 24-gauge metal wire to fashion a silver bird's nest, then fill it with white feathers. Look for metal initials at flea markets or have a silversmith craft them for a three-dimensional monogram cake topper. Place dollhouse-sized furnishings like a gazebo blooming with sugar flowers on the top floor of your cake, or crown it with a tiara of royal icing and pearly dragées.

favors, tosses, & keepsakes

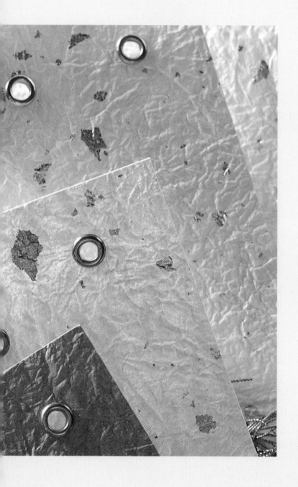

Tokens of affection come in many forms, from simple cellophane bags of candy to hand-embossed photo albums. These tiny gifts are meant to thank guests for sharing the joy of the day. They should never break the bank, but they should always be festive. In my experience, a bit of clever packaging makes a big impression. Couch confetti in cones rolled from origami paper or sheet music of favorite love songs, seal plain paper bags with seashells or feathers, tuck secret family recipes inside glassine sleeves. Whimsical touches will always be remembered, so toss white silk rose petals or fasten your favors with colorful sequined tags. And don't shy away from being sentimental. Accentuating your wedding program with snippets of personal history gives guests a glimpse into your love story, and makes them feel as if they're a part of it, too.

welcome bucket

My favorite wedding celebrations unfold over long weekends. Whether guests and family members return to your hometown or join you at another destination, it's considerate to welcome them with a token of affection that also includes some practical information. A welcome bucket, basket, or tote can be filled with a variety of items. I suggest adding a homemade snack, a map of the area, an itinerary with helpful phone numbers, and a fun accessory like a bandanna (make it de rigueur attire at one of the pre-wedding parties!). This bucket filled with beachy treats is perfect for a seaside celebration.

**Enamel-finished
decorative bucket**

Vintage postcard

Calligrapher marker (optional)

Glue stick (optional)

Local map

**3 x 4-inch cellophane bag,
available from confectionery
suppliers**

¼ cup light brown sugar

2 iced cookies

¹⁄₁₆-inch hole punch

8-inch length of twine

**Large decorative shell,
available at nautical gift shops**

Bottled water

Sunscreen

2 bandannas

2 pairs sunglasses

1. Hand-letter the weekend itinerary on the back of a vintage postcard depicting your celebration locale. Or type the itinerary on your computer, print out and trim the paper, then adhere to the back of the postcard with glue.

2. Find or create a map of the area. Local maps can be color-copied and laminated with important phone numbers and additional details.

3. To make the cookie pouch, pour a scant ¼ cup of brown sugar into the cellophane bag, then tuck in the iced cookies. Fold down the top of the bag about a half-inch. Use the hole punch to make a hole in the center of the fold, thread with the twine, and close with a nautical knot.

4. Fill the bucket with assorted items, such as a keepsake seashell, bottled water, sunscreen, a couple of bandannas, or two pairs of fun sunglasses. Then place one bucket as a welcome in each guest room.

Variations: Almost any clever container works as a welcome kit. Straw bags, hatboxes, acrylic boxes, galvanized lunch boxes, paper totes with ribbon straps, vinyl bags in bright colors—all are interesting options, and their handles make them easy to transport.

favor bags

Homemade confections—iced cookies, chocolate truffles, fudge brownies, peanut brittle—are always gratefully received, all the more so because they come from your kitchen. Tiny paper bags make perfect takeout pouches for baked goodies wrapped in wax paper. To personalize plain white bags, detail them with velvety ribbons, silvered tassels, wired pearls, or a single seashell.

Wax paper squares

Decorative round sticker

3½ x 5½-inch white paper bags, available at party suppliers

¹⁄₁₆-inch hole punch

9-inch length of ribbon

2-inch-long tassel

4-inch length 22-gauge wire

33 tiny ready-to-thread plastic pearls, available at bead and craft stores

2 ³⁄₈-inch pearls

Needle-nose pliers

5-inch length kraft-paper-wrapped wire, available at craft shops

2-inch decorative shell, available at nautical gift shops

5-inch-length 24-gauge wire

1. Wrap the baked goods in wax paper, seal with a decorative sticker, tuck them into the paper bag, and fold a one-inch flap at the top.
2. Use the hole punch to make two parallel holes through the flap.

For a ribboned bag, thread the ribbon through the holes, tie a bow, and loop the tassel's cord around the ribbon at the back of the bow.

To fasten with pearls, use the needle-nose pliers to twist a tiny knot at one end of the 22-gauge wire length. String the wire first with one of the large pearls, followed by all of the tiny pearls. Thread the wired strand through the holes, then string the other end with the remaining large pearl. Knot the wire end with the needle-nose pliers to secure, and then loosely twist the two ends around each other for a finishing touch.

To accent bags with a seashell, thread the kraft paper wire through the holes and twist to close at the back of the bag. Attach the shell to the kraft paper wire by wrapping it with the length of 24-gauge wire.

Variations: Mini paper bags also come in kraft and colorful papers. Use rubber stamps, stencils, a monogrammed label, grommets, silk butterflies, or wax seals to detail.

sweet favors

Candy, prettily colored and pleasing to taste, is always a welcome token of affection. After all, who doesn't have a sweet tooth? I find that these cheerful favors need little in the way of fancy packaging. Instead, I like to let their bright coatings shine through simple cellophane bags knotted with a swatch of ribbon. For sentimental reasons, old-fashioned candies are my first choice to give as favors. Couples might want to consider bundling up their own childhood favorites or sweets that reflect their cultural or geographic origins.

2 x 5-inch gusseted cellophane bags, available from confectionery suppliers

¼ cup candy per bag

8-inch lengths of ribbon, 1 per bag

Additional notions: beads, tags, wired paper leaves (optional)

1. Fill each cellophane bag with candy.
2. Knot each bag closed.
3. Tie a length of ribbon over each knot. Add additional notions to the ribbon to detail the bag as desired.

Variations: Pictured clockwise from the top: pink M&Ms, checked satin ribbon, pink feather; peppermint pillows, silk cord with beads; minty balls, rosebud ribbon; pink and white heart sprinkles, organza ribbon; turquoise sugarcoated almonds, satin ribbon, wired paper leaves; pastel dots, wired paper roses; conversation hearts, satin ribbon, hand-punched paper heart; silver sugarcoated chocolate hearts, strand of wired pearls.

MACHELL & AARONS
wedding feast

Uncle Jon's Garden Gazpacho ~ Aunt Bea's Cool Cucumber Soup

Aunt Francesca's Penne Pesto
Pete & Jason's Primavera Fettuccini
Grandma Miller's Three Potato Salad
Mesculin Salad with Katie's Vinaigrette

Grandma's World Famous Buttermilk Biscuits

Grilled Jumbo Shrimp with Alan's Bayou Salsa
Uncle Russ' Roasted Butterfly of Lamb

Grandma Shelly's Apricot Crisp ~ Aunt Jenny's Ph
Aunt Anna's Glazed Raspberry Pie ~ Aunt Nancy's
Aunt Alice's Rhubarb Crisp

a recipe selection from machell & a

Weddings held at home extend a familial embrace to all who cross the threshold. Kith and kin will delight in every ancestral photo and sentimental treasure on display. I suggest couples consider incorporating many domestic details into their celebration to underscore the emotional ties that bind. Compile a list of favorite songs for the musicians to perform and serve legendary family delicacies, then offer a vellum-wrapped packet of the recipes as a favor for all to keep.

Family recipes

Photo of the family home where the wedding is being held

8½ x 11-inch sheet of photocopy-weight vellum, available at stationery stores

Paper cutter

Ruler

Pencil

Bone folder

Glue stick

8½ x 11-inch heavyweight bond paper for photocopies

1. Gather the recipes you want to include in the packet and rewrite them in a handsome but legible script to fit within a 4 x 6-inch format. Don't forget to name the family member who originated the dish: Aunt Mabel's Corn Bread Pudding, for example.

2. Use a computer program to list all the recipes in a menu format. Allow a one-inch margin at the top and sides, and position the text so that it will print centered in the top half of a 8½ x 6-inch sheet of vellum. Print out a template and photocopy on the vellum. This will become the sleeve for the packet of recipes.

3. Use the paper cutter to trim the vellum to 8½ x 6 inches.

4. Measure in one inch from the left margin of the vellum and lightly mark with pencil. Make a vertical fold at this mark along the entire length of the vellum.

5. Measure in four inches from the top of the vellum and lightly mark with pencil. Make a horizontal fold at this mark along the entire length of the vellum. There will be a half-inch extension of vellum: Fold it under to create a horizontal flap for the sleeve.

6. Use the bone folder to permanently crease the three folds, then seal the flaps with glue and smooth over the glued seams with the bone folder. This sleeve will measure 4 x 6 inches.

7. Photocopy the image of the family home on bond paper. Use the paper cutter to trim to a 3⅝ x 5⅝-inch postcard. The card should be slightly smaller than the sleeve so that it fits snugly, but without too much extra room. Insert the card into the vellum sleeve so that the image appears behind the menu.

8. Photocopy the recipes on bond paper. Use the paper cutter to trim each one into a 3⅝ x 5⅝-inch postcard. Insert the recipe cards underneath the postcard of the family home.

favor tags

Because wedding favors are obviously being given by the couple to all of their guests, these tokens of affection need only the simplest tags. A label might even seem superfluous, although it is helpful when the favor is also being used as a place card at the table setting. I often find that a trip to the stationer's yields a treasure trove of ideas for label looks: sophisticated stickers, decorative hole punches, rubber stamps. And your average office supply store offers paper tags in a variety of styles. I always replace the basic strings attached to these tags with ribbons, cords, even wired strands of plastic pearls.

Assorted tags or gift cards, available at office supply or stationery stores

Decorative hole punch or die-cut

Stickers

Hand-embosser with initial or artwork plate, available to order from specialty stationers or art supply stores

Assorted calligraphy markers

Ribbons or cords

Beads

Wired plastic pearls

Scissors

1. Select a style of tag. When making your choice, take into account such factors as the weight and color of the paper, the shape of the tag, and the size of the tag in proportion to the favor.
2. Detail the tags using one or more of the following techniques: Stamp with a hole punch or die-cut in the shape of a flower, heart, letter, or other symbol. Add textured stickers like velvety maple leaves and daisies or adhesive crystals and sequins. Emboss with initials or the date—for the large tag in the upper left of the photo, I stamped a metallic notary seal with the letter M using a custom-ordered embossing tool.
3. Address the tags with calligraphy markers.
4. String the tags with ribbons, beaded cords, or wired pearl strands.

Variations: Silk-screen fabric swatches with an original design. Hand-letter wired paper leaves or flowers or Mexican stamped tin ornaments, which are available in the shape of hearts, suns, moons, and other engaging symbols. Ribbons in various fabrics can be embroidered or printed to order metal "dog tags" can be stamped with a message. Plastic suppliers will cut acrylic discs to size, drill with a small hole, and etch with lettering or the date of the wedding.

feather tosses

Showering couples with confetti is an exuberant show of affection, a gesture delightful to give and receive. This playful accessory can take many forms, comprised of two main components: the confetti and a container to keep it in. Sheet music of favorite songs make whimsical paper cones. I fill them with fanciful white feathers that seem to float like musical notes through the air when thrown. To display the scrolls, arrange them in a proper silver punch bowl.

8½ x 11-inch page of sheet music

Craft glue

Scissors

Glue gun

12-inch length of ¼-inch-wide satin ribbon

Metal medallion, available at craft stores

White feathers, available at craft stores

Silver punch bowl

1. Roll the sheet music into a cone. Draw a bead of craft glue along the inside edge of the outer flap to bond the paper into position. Use a few dots of glue on the inside of the cone to bond the inner flap. Fold up a one-inch flap at the base of the cone and use glue to seal.

2. Wrap the ribbon around the top of the cone about an inch below the opening. Secure the ribbon in place with a dot of craft glue. Trim the ribbon ends with scissors to leave an inch-and-a-half tail on both sides.

3. Use the glue gun to anchor the medallion to the cross point of the ribbon.

4. Fill the cone with feathers.

5. Spread a layer of feathers in the base of the punch bowl, then nest all the finished cones in the bowl. Add more loose feathers between the cones.

eleven tosses

It's considered good luck—and lots of fun—to shower newlyweds with confetti. Almost any lightweight material cut small can be thrown. But many locations limit the use of some tosses due to liability concerns—for example, rice can be slippery on stairs—or worries about attracting unwanted guests, as is often the case with birdseed and pigeons, so find out your location's preferences beforehand. I love to fill glassine envelopes with a colorful confetti like blue feathers, then top them with escort cards so that they serve a dual function.

Calligraphy marker

Escort card

2 x 3-inch glassine envelope

Handful of confetti

¹⁄₁₆-inch hole punch

6-inch length of ribbon

1. Use the calligraphy marker to hand-letter the card with the guest name on the front, the table number on the reverse.
2. Fill the glassine envelope with a handful of confetti.
3. Stack the escort card on top of the envelope. Punch a hole through the top center of the envelope, and another hole directly below it through the top center of the envelope and the card.
4. Thread the ribbon through both sets of holes and tie with a simple knot. For an envelope filled with feathers, tuck an extra feather into the ribbon knot, as shown.

Variations: Confetti options, pictured left to right, top to bottom: dried lavender; birdseed; pale blue feathers; reflective Mylar confetti; letter-pressed paper confetti; birdseed; puffed polyester hearts; white silk petals; opalescent Mylar confetti; baby's breath buds; fennel seeds.

origami cones

I've always admired the thick, textured papers used by origami artists to create beautiful objects. In fact, these delightful papers have many decorative uses. Prepackaged squares are ready to roll into cones that hold birdseed or other confetti. A few grommet rings secure the paper in place, and a frayed cord adorns the base. The top of the cone is meant to remain open, so that with a wave of the hand guests can spray the couple with the confetti. To limit spillage, don't distribute cones until immediately before the toss. Have ushers stand with trays or baskets of cones to offer guests as they exit the ceremony and wait for the newlyweds to appear.

6-inch square of origami paper

Grommet kit containing ⅛-inch grommet tool and grommet rings, available at hardware stores

6-inch length of braided cord thin enough to thread through the grommet holes

⅓ cup birdseed or other confetti

1. Roll the sheet of origami paper into a cone.
2. Follow the instructions on the kit to punch a grommet hole into the throat of the cone. The grommet ring will fasten the two layers of paper together.
3. Fold up a ¾-inch flap at the base of the cone and punch a grommet hole through it to fasten in place.
4. Punch a third grommet hole into the extended point of the paper for decoration.
5. Thread the braided cord through the grommet hole at the base of the cone. To secure, tie a simple knot in the cord on both sides of the hole. Fray the ends of the cord for a softer finish.
6. Fill the cone with birdseed or the confetti of your choice.

rustic fans

Offering guests at a summer wedding a fan that doubles as a favor is a smart and thoughtful gesture. With the help of a hand-laminator, it's possible to transform a wide range of artwork or maps into durable and water-resistant objects. Adhered to rustic twigs and placed in mason jars filled with stones, they make Zen-like arrangements for outdoor tables.

5 x 7-inch chipboard panel

5 x 7-inch copy of a topographical map that features the wedding location

5 x 7-inch page of the wedding program text

Hand-laminator kit, available at craft and office supply stores

Cutting board

Utility knife

Ruler

15-inch-long, ¼-inch-thick twig

Screw punch, also known as a Japanese push drill

4 2-inch lengths 20-gauge wire

Wire cutters

Craft glue

Tiny pinecone

Mason jar

Stones

Large stone

Permanent marker

Highlighter pen or small adhesive star

1. Highlight the exact location of the wedding on the map with a dot or a star.
2. Sandwich the chipboard panel between the map and the wedding program, placing both pieces of paper front side out. Feed the package through the laminator according to the kit instructions to seal the three components into a single item, with the map legible on one side, the program on the other.
3. On the cutting board, use the utility knife and the ruler to trim the plastic to ⅛-inch around the laminated page.
4. Lay the twig on top of the map side of the laminated page to determine a naturalistic placement. Ideally, it will rest at a slight angle and cover about two-thirds of the page. Use the screw punch to flank the twig with four pairs of holes, equally spaced.
5. Thread one length of wire through a pair of holes and around the twig, twist the ends of the wire together to secure, and trim any excess. Repeat for each pair of holes to attach the twig to the page.
6. Use a dab of craft glue to adhere the pinecone to the twig at the base of the map.
7. Insert the fan in the mason jar. One jar will hold about 12 fans. Once all the fans have been added, fill the jar with stones.
8. Station the fans near the entrance point to the seating area for an outdoor wedding. Place more stones around the base of the jar and use the permanent marker to label the large stone with your names and wedding date.

family album

On a day that celebrates hope for a happy future, it's only fitting to reflect upon the past. An accordion-style booklet with pages displaying portraits of previous generations of family brides is a sentimental favor. Color copiers make fine reproductions of old photos, which I mount on card stock. For the cover, seek out richly embossed or textured papers that invite touch.

2 panels 12 x 4-inch, deckled-edge, 60-pound card stock, available at specialty stationers

8½ x 11-inch sheet 80-pound embossed paper, available at specialty stationers

2-foot length of ¼-inch-wide satin ribbon

11 family photos

Paper cutter

Ruler

Bone folder

Glue stick

Calligraphy marker

⅛-inch hole punch

Scissors

1. Work with a color photocopier to reduce or enlarge the family photos to 2½ x 3½ inches. To economize, fit more than one image on a standard-sized sheet of paper when copying. Trim the photocopies with the paper cutter.

2. Use the ruler and the bone folder to crease the two long panels into accordion pages that measure 3 x 4 inches.

3. Line up the last page of one accordion panel with the first page of the other and glue together back to front to create one long accordion panel with seven pages.

4. Trim the sheet of embossed paper into two 3 x 4-inch rectangles. Align one rectangle on top of the first accordion page and glue in place for the front cover. Align and glue the other rectangle on top of the last accordion page for the back cover.

5. The booklet will now consist of six pages on either side, for a total of 12 pages. On the first or last page (the one glued to the front or back cover), list the brides and their wedding dates.

6. Organize the 11 photocopied portraits to match the list. Center each portrait on a page. Adhere with the glue stick.

7. Along the outside edge of the front and back covers, punch a hole at the center point. (Note that this hole will also pass through the list of names at one end of the booklet and a portrait at the other.)

8. With the ruler and scissors, measure, then cut the ribbon into one 10-inch length and one 14-inch length. Thread the 10-inch length through the hole in the front cover. Tie in a simple slipknot. Thread the 14-inch length through the hole in the back cover, slipknot, then wrap the strands around the entire folded booklet and tie a loose bow to close. Tuck the ends of the shorter ribbon into the band encircling the booklet.

embossed programs

Fashion a smart booklet from colorful paper, bind it with silky ribbon, and emboss the cover to give an artisan's finish to the missal. Any artwork can be made into a hand-embosser, but letters or symbols with simple lines translate the best. I asked a calligrapher to design an initial that could be used for the programs and also on coasters, tags, and stationery.

Hand-embosser with initial or artwork plate, available to order from specialty stationers or art supply stores

8½ x 11-inch, 80-pound cover stock, 1 sheet per booklet

8½ x 11-inch, 30-pound text paper, 2 sheets for a 4-page booklet

Bone folder

Ruler

Pencil

Screw punch, also known as a Japanese push drill

7-inch length of 1-inch-wide silk ribbon

1. At least two weeks in advance, order the hand-embosser. Because the tools have a four-inch reach and most can be impressed in one direction only, it's important to determine your layout beforehand. You'll need to provide artwork for the plate. If you've hired a professional to create it, add another four weeks to the schedule.

2. Compose your text on computer. The first page should be a title page, the interior pages provide information in chronological order, and the last page can feature a poem, artwork, or simply the date. Arrange text for the interior pages in two columns, and note that the paper will be positioned horizontally: The 11-inch sides will be folded in half to create 5½ x 8½-inch pages. When formatting your text, allow room for the ribbon spine. And also note that you'll be printing different pages of text on the same sheet of paper. For example, in a four-page booklet, the text for pages 2 and 7 should print on one side of the same sheet, with the text for pages 1 and 8 printing on the back of that same sheet. This way, when you layer the pages, the text will read in the proper order.

3. Print, fold, and tuck the pages in order, one inside another.

4. Fold the cover stock in half so that it measures 5½ x 8½ inches. Run the bone folder across the crease to press. Open the sheet. Use the ruler and pencil to measure and mark spots for two holes set one inch apart in the center on the crease. Screw-punch out the two holes. Using the cover as a guide, punch identically placed holes in the stack of text paper. When all the sheets have been punched, refold and go over each crease with the bone folder.

5. Position the embosser so that the plate is centered above the front cover. Press firmly for 10 seconds to emboss.

6. Insert the text booklet inside the cover. Thread the holes with the ribbon to bind the pages, and tie on the outside in a simple knot.

wedding signs

I believe a message commands more attention when it's expressed through an appealing design. This final chapter doesn't stray from my mantra. The details count, even when merely pointing the way. Paying attention to the seemingly most mundane aspects of your wedding day *will* make a difference. Consider, for example, traffic control. Clear directionals are a necessity, and will be greatly appreciated by guests driving down rural roads in search of a well-hidden reception site. In their own small fashion, signs are the very first markers of the celebration to come, and they help to set the tone. So for country weddings, keep signposts rustic by crafting them from rough-hewn planks, and at more modern affairs, don't string plain soup cans from the trunk of your getaway car: Spray-paint them silver. But no matter how you choose to style your signs, the joyful message will still be the same: Just Married!

rustic directional sign

Country weddings will always be popular because the locations are quaint and bucolic. I suggest couples include a map with the invitation and direct guests to take the scenic route to the destination. If the reception site really feels like it's in the middle of nowhere, with few obvious landmarks to indicate the way, it's helpful to post signage along the roads to signal where to turn. I find rough-hewn pine makes an appropriately rustic directional.

5-foot-long, 4 x 4-inch pine post

4 30-inch lengths of 1 x 4-inch pine planks

2 15-inch lengths of 5 x 1-inch pine stripping

8 1-inch wood screws

2 3-inch wood screws

Pencil

Ruler

Drill

Circular saw

Cotton rag

Paintbrush

Plastic tub

½ cup white paint

½ pint black paint

Shovel

1. With a pencil, mark the one-, five-, nine-, and 13-inch points along the two lengths of stripping. Drill holes.

2. Line up the four planks facedown. Position the two lengths of stripping perpendicularly across the backs of the planks. Place them about 20 inches apart, and align them so that the two rows of four holes both match up with the four planks. Drill through the holes into the planks with the inch-long wood screws to secure.

3. Use the circular saw to cut one end of the planks into a point.

4. To distress the face of the pine, mix white paint one to one with water in the plastic tub, then dip the cotton rag into the diluted solution and swipe the wood in a haphazard manner. Distress the post at the same time. When dry, use the paintbrush to write "The Wedding" in black paint on the sign.

5. Attach the sign to the post with the three-inch wood screws.

6. Dig a hole about a foot and a half deep in which to plant the post.

Variations: Although barns, wineries, and informal at-home receptions are best represented by rustic materials like barnwood, use etched acrylics or peel-and-stick decals on brightly painted wood for a modern edge. But keep the lettering big and clear, and eliminate any excess ornamentation: The important thing is that the signs are easy for drivers to read. For nighttime events, dark letters over white paint or the reverse provide the most legible contrast.

barnwood sign

While June brides will never go out of style, autumn is an increasingly popular season in which to wed. Fall foliage provides a gloriously vivid backdrop, and the promise of temperate eves, compared to steamy summer days, practically guarantees that cooler heads will prevail. For couples planning a celebration at a farm, country inn, or vineyard, a "Just Married" sign crafted from scrap wood makes a charming accent.

2 x 3-foot, ⅜-inch-thick,
rough-cut plywood plank

½ pint birch paint

Plastic tub

Cotton rag

Pencil

Butane welding torch

Drill with ⅜-inch bit

Fine-grade sandpaper

3-foot length of rough twine

2 2-foot lengths of celadon
organza ribbon

4 stems seeded eucalyptus

1. In the plastic tub, mix the half-pint of birch paint with a half-pint of water. Dip the cotton rag in the mixture, then wipe it across the plywood plank to "weather" it. Let dry. Repeat.

2. Pencil the words "Just Married" on the plank to determine the appropriate size and placement for the letters.

3. Ignite the butane torch according to the instructions printed on the container.

4. Follow the pencil marks and use steady, patient pressure to burn the letters into the plywood. When done, singe the perimeter of the plank to frame the message.

5. About three inches from the top and five inches in from the sides of the plank, drill a pair of holes. Use the sandpaper to smooth any splintered edges.

6. Thread the twine through the holes and knot to hang at the desired length. Tie a loose organza bow around the twine above the holes, and tuck sprigs of eucalyptus into the ribbon knots.

"just married" wreath

Charming signage usually hangs from the back of the newlyweds' car, but an oversized version scrawled in loopy script and framed by a verdant wreath makes a cheerful addition to the reception décor, too, especially when the party is taking place at a homey locale. For a wedding at a family farm, I asked a favorite calligrapher to letter the words "Just Married" on a large square of drawing paper. Then I crafted a wreath out of maple, cedar, and blueberry branches. Fastened to a freshly whitewashed barn door, the autumnal foliage made a dramatic banner.

30-inch square of heavyweight drawing paper

Calligraphy markers

20 bunches maple leaf branches

10 bunches cedar leaf branches

10 bunches wild blueberry leaf branches

10 bunches grapes

5 bunches eucalyptus berries

Spool 20-gauge dark green florist wire

45-inch wreath ring, available at craft and floral suppliers

Clippers

Tape meaure

Needle-nose pliers

Hole punch

Scissors

Spool nylon monofilament

1. Use calligraphy markers to letter the drawing paper as desired.
2. The day before the wedding, gather the maple, cedar, and blueberry branches along with the eucalyptus berries at your workstation. To start, twist and knot one end of florist wire to the wreath ring. Do not cut the wire from the spool, simply unfurl short lengths as needed to attach foliage. Arrange the foliage in small mixed bundles and wire them by their stems to the frame. Layer bundle upon bundle of foliage to fill out the wreath. When the wreath is covered, clip the wire from the spool and twist the end into the frame. Fill any bare spots with individually wired bundles and bits of foliage.
3. Cut a five-foot length of florist wire. Fold up each end of the wire at the 10-inch mark and prepare to hang the wreath from these "hooks." Thread each hook through the back of the wreath, one at the same point on either side, just above the center. Use the needle-nose pliers to twist the 10-inch segments tightly around the longer lengths of wire to securely support the weight of the wreath.
4. Just before hanging the wreath, use four-inch lengths of florist wire to attach grape clusters to the front of it.
5. Punch a hole in each corner of the sign and attach it to the back of the wreath with short lengths of monofilament so that the words can be read through the center of the wreath.

Variations: Hang smaller versions of the wreath from the back of the getaway car. For winter wreaths, work with evergreens; in summer, try sunflowers or dried hydrangea heads. Change the selection of foliage to match the season and the palette of your celebration.

"just married" flags

Paper pennants lettered with the joyful words "Just Married" and detailed with a sweet illustration make charming cocktail party centerpieces. I've also handed these happy banners to guests so that they can cheer "Bon Voyage!" as the newlyweds depart, and I've attached them to the radio antennas of all the cars in the bridal entourage. It's not often that you literally get to wave your own flag, so make the most of the opportunity!

60-pound cover weight paper stock in your favorite color, trimmed into an 8 x 10 x 10-inch triangle

Calligraphy markers or paints in a variety of colors, or access to a computer design program

Paper cutter

Glue stick

18-inch-long, ⅛-inch-round dowel

8-inch length of 2-inch-wide satin ribbon in a color that matches the art

2 1-yard lengths of ¹⁄₁₆-inch-wide satin ribbon

Bone folder

Vase

Gerber daisies

1. Use markers, paints, or a computer program to create artwork for your pennant. Draft an original design that includes your names and an illustration—ask artistic friends for help, or hire a professional. The design should fit comfortably within the parameters of the paper triangle. Aim to center the artwork, so that both sides of the flag will match up when sealed together.

2. Make color photocopies of the artwork. You'll need two copies per flag. Use the paper cutter to trim the pages into triangles.

3. Draw a thin line of glue down the center of the wide satin ribbon. Align one end of the dowel with the top of the ribbon and lay it down the center, in the line of glue, to adhere. Wrap the sides of the ribbon around the dowel and draw another thin line of glue along the inside of the fabric. Press the sides of the ribbon together to seal. The resulting tab of ribbon will be used to attach the two paper triangles.

4. Place one triangle facedown at your workstation. Draw a thin line of glue along the short, vertical side of the triangle. Position the dowel so that the ribboned end becomes the spine of the flag. Press into the glue to adhere. Draw another thin line of glue in the same place on a second triangle, position on top of the dowel, and press to adhere. The two triangles should now sandwich the ribboned section of the dowel.

5. Check that the horizontal points of the two triangles align, then seal the triangles together all along the inside edges of the paper with glue. Smooth with the bone folder.

6. Knot the thin satin ribbon lengths at their midpoint around the dowel at the base of the flag. Insert the dowel into the vase of daisies and arrange the ribbon streamers on the tabletop.

"just married" decal

Tradition dictates that newlyweds dash off in a vehicle that's been lettered with the cheerful declaration "Just Married!" But I admit I've always found it challenging to decorate cars. Their round backs tend to bump signs hung from the fender, and tailwinds often end up tearing apart the handiwork anyway. During a visit to my favorite plastic supplier, I found sheets of silver peel-and-stick Mylar. The material is easy to cut, it adheres to glass, and it can be removed with a nonabrasive solvent. The vendor also sold Mylar curtains, so I clamped one in the trunk for a festive fringe that waved a shiny "So long!" as the bride and groom drove away.

15 x 24-inch sheet of peel-and-stick Mylar, available at plastic suppliers

4-foot-wide Mylar curtain

8½ x 11-inch sheets of tracing paper

Pencil

Scotch tape

Scissors

Duct tape

Goo Gone or other nonabrasive solvent

Paper towels

1. Pencil sheets of tracing paper with whatever words you want to use in your decal. Depending on the size of your prospective decal, you may be able to fit just one letter or an entire word on one sheet of paper.
2. Scotch-tape the tracing paper over the shiny side of the Mylar and use scissors to cut out your lettering. Many plastic suppliers will also laser-cut artwork or lettering to your specifications.
3. Peel off the protective backing and stick the Mylar lettering to the center of the car window.
4. Open the trunk, lay the Mylar curtain over the bottom edge, and attach the top of the curtain to the inside of the trunk with duct tape. Close the trunk. Use scissors to trim the length of the curtain as desired.
5. To remove the lettering, squirt with the nonabrasive solvent and peel off. Apply more solvent as needed, and wipe the window clean with paper towels.

silvered cans

Tying tin cans to the newlyweds' car may seem to be a particularly American custom, but the belief that noisemakers can ward off evil spirits and announce happy news exists in many different cultures around the world. Because I obsess about every last detail, one day I decided to add a touch of class to common soup cans by spray-painting them silver and stringing them on satin ribbons. Ever since then, plain cans have seemed . . . well, underdressed!

20 soup-sized tin cans

1 yard of 2-inch-wide satin ribbon per can

Can silver spray paint

Rotating can opener

Hammer

Awl

Blunt-nosed chisel

Large cardboard box

Duct tape

1. If you haven't already, rinse out the cans and remove any labels. Leave the bottom of the can intact, but use the rotating can opener to completely sever any partially attached top lids. Discard or recycle the lids, and hammer flat any sharp edges around the mouth of the can.

2. Tap the awl with the hammer to punch a hole in the center of the closed bottom end of each can. Flatten any sharp edges on the inside of the can with the blunt-nosed chisel.

3. In a well-ventilated area, place the cans in the cardboard box and spray-paint. After an initial coating, toss the cans in the box to check for any missed spots, then spray again. Let dry. Cans can be painted weeks in advance.

4. Thread a yard of ribbon through the hole in each can. Tie the threaded end in a tight double knot so that the ribbon won't slip out.

5. Tie the cans into bunches of five, knotting together the free ends of ribbon approximately five inches down the length.

6. Assign someone to hang the cans from the trunk of the getaway car during the ceremony. Use six-inch strips of duct tape to attach each bunch of cans to the inside lip of the trunk. Space the bunches of cans about five inches apart along the rim of the trunk. Once the trunk is closed a lively fringe of ribboned cans will trail along the ground.

Variations: Use a metallic fabric marker to letter the ribbons with the message: Just Married!

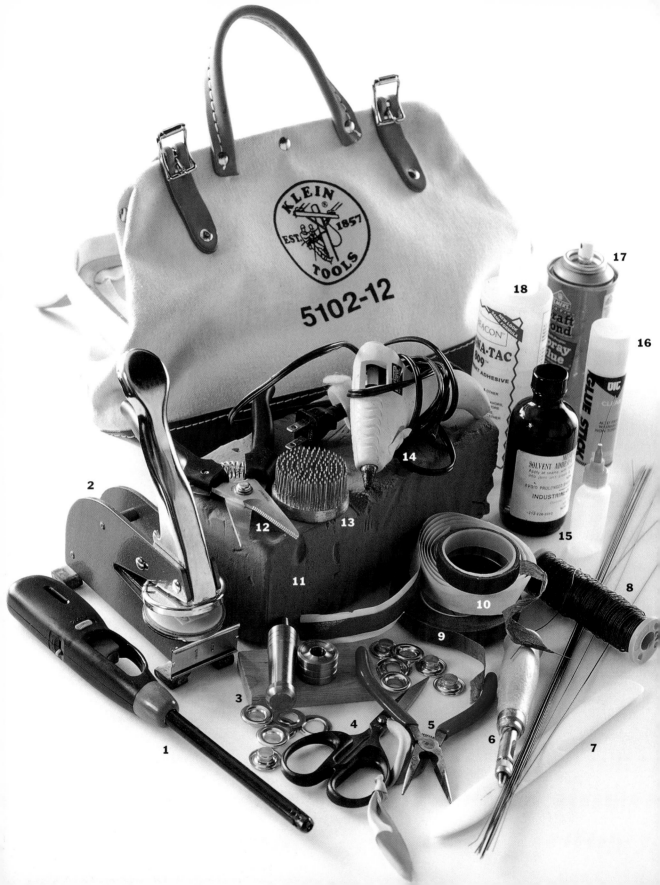

To create the projects in this book I relied over and over again on these basic tools to complete each recipe. Here are the indispensable items that I always keep handy in my craft bag.

1. Butane torch. The trigger and long snout make it easy to light dozens of votives within minutes. Stock several, and enlist help for quick lighting. Available at grocery stores.

2. Hand-embosser. This tool makes it easy to emboss a menu, program, place card, or favor with a monogram. Allow two weeks to order; once in hand you'll discover dozens of uses for the tool. Available through stationery suppliers.

3. Grommet kit. This tiny kit handles the big job of creating metal-ringed holes in a variety of fabrics; use the tool to make corsets, curtains, and canopies. Grommet tools are widely available from ⅛ inch to 2 inches at hardware stores.

4. Scissors. Reserve one medium-sized pair for ribbons only. To cut smoothly, you need sheers with a clean, sharp edge. A knot of ribbon on the handle marks it "ribbons only."

5. Needle-nose pliers. A versatile tool, I use it to twist the ends of wires together and to make decorative curls. Available at hardware or bead shops.

6. Screw punch or **Japanese push drill.** Unlike traditional hole punches that limit cuts to the reach of the handle, this has a sharp, circular tip that allows holes to be cut anywhere. Available at book binding and craft suppliers.

7. Bone folder. A book binder's tool that is used to rub creases into papers, its pointed edge is useful for pushing out fabric corners. Available at book binding and art suppliers.

8. Florist wires. Dark green, it's sold as 14-inch stems or on a spool. It is not meant to be seen; its color allows it to blend into the project or bouquet. Wire is available in a variety of thicknesses or gauges. Glue 18-gauge, the thickness of spaghetti, to heavier objects like sea shells; 22-gauge, the thickness of angel hair pasta, is best for bead work or boutonnieres. Craft shops stock similar gauge wires in brass and silver for decorative detailing.

9. Florist tape. Elasticized paper tape spools are available in green or white and are used for wiring stems of flowers or boutonnieres. Available at florist supply shops.

10. Florist clay. This dark green putty is impervious to water and removable. I use wads to secure frogs to the inside of vases. Available at florist suppliers on a handy tape spool or by the brick.

11. Oasis. Foam bricks that can hold 10 times their weight in water; hence its name. Wet foam keeps stems happy and allows varied arrangement shapes. Oasis foam also comes in small plastic cages or domes, useful for pomanders or any small arrangement.

12. Flower clippers. Find a pair that feels good in your hands and keep them clean and sharp for the best results. All flowers should be conditioned properly—that's the real key to a beautiful arrangement—because fresh flowers need their stems cut at least two inches and immediately plunged into a bucket of water to drink for a day before designing.

13. Frogs. Available in many sizes, the metal teeth provide a secure anchor and precise placement of the stem. Use a wad of floral clay to anchor the frog to the bottom of a vase or saucer before arranging with blooms. Available at floral and garden suppliers.

14. Glue gun. An electric tool for melting glue sticks, which are inserted into the barrel. Handle this tool and objects that are dabbed with glue gingerly; the metal tip becomes very hot and the melted glue can scald your fingertips. Widely available at hardware and craft shops.

15. Solvent adhesive. Adheres acrylics together because the adhesive dissolves the plastic to create a bond when dry. A needle-nose applicator allows precise application. Available at plastic supply shops.

16. Glue stick. Fabulous, mess-free way to adhere papers, including photographs. Aim for a thin smear of glue for a smooth finish. Widely available in arts and crafts stores.

17. Spray adhesive. Covers large areas with a sticky film that stays tacky for hours, allowing plenty of time to complete projects. Available at hardware and craft shops.

18. Craft adhesive. Great for attaching beads to fabrics or trimmings to glass. Available at craft and fabric shops.

resources

Here is a list of some of my favorite providers, services, and sources for producing the projects featured in this book. For hundreds of additional listings of important resources for wedding planning, please see my other books, *The Perfect Wedding* and *The Perfect Wedding Reception*. Direct any questions, suggestions, or changes for this list to my attention at MariaMcBride.com.

ART & CRAFTS SUPPLIES

All Season Trading Company
Allseason.com
415-864-3308
wide variety of beads

Artstore.com
415-441-6075
screen printing supplies

Auntie's Beads
Auntiesbeads.com
866-26-BEADS
lots of beads

Beaded Impressions
Abeadstore.com
303-442-3473
beads and jewelry notions

Exposures
888-345-6693
exposuresonline.com
archival, photo supplies

Gettinger Feather
gettingerfeather.com
212-695-9470
assorted feathers, colors

Harper Imports
773-268-6840
glass leaves, beads

Industrial Plastics Supply Co.
212-226-2010
plastics, Mylars, custom
fabrications

Jo-ann Fabrics & Crafts
888-739-4120
www.joann.com

Light Impressions
lightimpressionsdirect.com
800-828-6216
metallic tape, archival supplies

Metalliferous
metalliferous.com
888-944-0909
metal mesh, wire, tools

New York Central Art Supply
nycentralart.com
800-950-6111
assorted papers, art tools

Pearl Paint
pearlpaint.com
800-451-PEARL
all art supplies

Sam Flax
samflax.com
800-SAM-FLAX
art supplies

Sepp Leaf
seppleaf.com
metal leaf, supplies

Set Shop
setshop.com
800-422-7381
photographic gels, Mylar and
diffusion paper

Swarovski Crystal
Swarovski.com
800-463-0211
crystal transfer appliqués, custom
design available

CALLIGRAPHY

Stephannie Barba
Stephanniebarba.com

Gail Brill Design
GailBrillDesign.com
203-869-4667

Calligraphic Arts
214-522-4731

Calligraphy Studios
212-964-6007

The Delicate Pen
212-877-3959

Karin Gable
818-343-2402

Nancy Howell
ragandboneshop.com
212-243-5804

Caroline Paget Leake
718-486-6844

Bernard Maisner
212-447-6776

Heather Belle McQuale
804-286-2940

Pendragon Ink
508-234-6843

Anna Pinto
201-656-7402

Prose & Letters
proseandletters.com
408-293-1852

Society of Scribes
societyofscribes.org
212-452-0139
information and referrals

XYZ Ink
XYZink.com

CANDLES &
LIGHTING

Beeskep II
beeskep2.com
518-762-5578
beeswax candles, many shapes

Casa Allegra
888-285-9907
iron candelabra

Creative Candles
creativecandles.com
800-237-9711
floating candles

Illuminations Candles
illuminations.com
800-226-3537
candles and candle holders

Paul Ashley
404-872-3971
Paul-ashley.com
candle holders, gifts

Robb Steck
robbsteck.com
650-367-1467
patterned candles

Table Décor International
tabledecor.com
800-265-5267
candle lamps and shades

Tokoloshe
416-663-8558
African-style painted candles

Wicks & Sticks
wicksnsticks.com
888-55-WICKS
retail candle shops

Zodax
zodax.com
decorative candles

CEREMONIAL
SUPPLIES

Angelthreads
718-462-0478
angelthreadsnyc.com
bridal accessories

The Artist Wedding Studio
chuppah.com
631-537-8008
custom chuppahs

Dazian Design Studio
dazian.com
212-206-3515
aisle runners, tent covers

Drape Kings
drapekings.com
888-DRAPE-ME
custom drapings

Lerica
212-279-3929
ring pillows

CONFECTIONARY
SUPPLIES

Alumart & Gifts
alumartandgifts.com
305-481-2235
Italian sugar pearls

Bob's Candies
Bobscandies.com
800-569-4033
white and classic
peppermint canes

Can You Imagine That
canyouimaginethat.com
877-643-8922
sand candy

Chef's Shop
877-337-2491
Chefshop.com
sugars, all colors

Dominosugar.com
Information, recipes, sugars

Dryden & Palmer Rock Candy Co.
rockcandy.com
203-481-3725
rock sugar on string, sticks

Economy Candy
economycandy.com
800-352-4544

Elenis Cookies
Elenis.com
212-255-7990
iced cookies

Gloria's Cake and Candy Supplies
gloriascakecandysuplys.com
310-391-4557
confectionary items

Hammond Candies
hammondscandies.com
888-CANDY-99
lollipops, ribbon candy, rock candy

Heatheryby's Delightful Cookies
503-328-0040
iced cookies for favors

McKandy
McKandy.com
888-525-7577
retro favorites

New York Cake & Baking Distributors
800-942-2539
rock sugars, all colors

Pastry Chef
pastrychef.com
561-999-1282
tools, pyramid molds

Pfeil & Holling
Cakedeco.com
800-247-7955
sugars, tools

Sugar Bouquets
sugarbouquets.com
800-203-0629
sugar flowers

Sugar Flowers Plus
sugarflowers.com
800-972-2935
sugar flowers, leaves

Tea and Cake Confections
teaandcake.com
naturally flavored lollipops

Williams-Sonoma
williams-sonoma.com
800-541-2233
kitchen and baking supplies

CONFETTIS

Design Ideas
designid.com
800-426-6394
metal star confetti

DHP Papermill & Press
dhproductions.net
845-228-5926
personalized letterpress confetti

Flutter Fetti
flutterfetti.com
877-321-1999
confetti tubes

Gettinger Feathers
Gettinger.com
212-695-9470
feathers, all colors

PANY
212-645-9526
silk rose petals, puffed heart confetti

Photo Confetti
photoconfetti.com

Pressed Petals
pressedpetals.com
800-748-4656
dried-flower-confetti, pressed flowers

SKD Trading
800-1 LUV-SKD
Mylar confetti

Wedding Flowers and More
weddingflowersandmore.com
silk petals

Xstreamers
xstreamers.com
888-925-7699
confetti streamers

DECORATIVE ACCESSORIES

American Home and Habitat
Americanhomeandhabitat.com
866-458-2559
netting, canopies, canvas

Artifacts
artifactsinc.com
800-678-4178
chandelier crystal

A Rustic Garden
Arusticgarden.com
217-773-3766
iron gazebos, screens

Charleston Gardens
charlestongardens.com
800-469-0118
fountains, furniture

Ebay.com
everything

Grand Brass Lamp Parts
212-226-2567
brass plates

Ikea
www.ikea.com
800-434-IKEA

Istanbul Grand Bazaar
istanbulgrandbazaar.com
212-799-7662

Midwest of Cannon Falls
midwestofcannonfalls.com
800-776-2075
ornaments and decorative objects

Moroccan Living
moroccanliving.com

Nicamakas
buyhammocks.com
866-377-1224
mosquito netting canopies

R and B Imports
randbimports.com
877-542-4551
capiz shell garlands

Schylling
Schylling.com
800-541-2929
enamel buckets

Smith & Hawken
800-776-3336
smithandhawken.com
decorative garden objects

Still Life
800-211-2511
metal leaf ornaments

Target
Target.com
patio heaters

Umbrellatime.com
800-316-9468
garden & thatched umbrellas

ETHNIC
NOVELTIES

A Thousand Cranes
athousandcranes.com
origami ornaments

Berberimports.com
Moroccan imports

CMC Company
thecmccompany.com
800-CMC-2780
hard-to-find ethnic foodstuffs

Cultural intrigue.com
800-799-7422
paper parasols, lanterns

e-mosaik.com
Moroccan decorative objects,
rentals, too

**Golden Gate Buddhist
Supplies**
212-233-3838
ceramics, incense, altars

Imports From Marrakesh
importsfrommarrakesh.com

Japanese Gifts
japanesegifts.com
877-226-4387
colorful paper lanterns and fans

Lee Carter Tzin Tzan Tzun
leecartercompany.com
Latin American novelties

Little India Stores
212-683-1691
diya heart candles

Magickware
Magickware.com
818-881-0827
cowrie shells, metaphysical gems

OCB Trading Post
Ocbtp.com
626-914-0306
Native American artifacts

Pearl River Mart
pearlriver.com
800-878-2446
Chinese novelties, porcelain

Sendleis.com
609-720-0300
fresh leis, express delivery

Wedding Sutra
weddingsutra.com
Indian traditions

FABRICS AND
NOTIONS

Britex Fabrics
britexfabrics.com
415-392-2910
fabrics and notions

Jo-ann Fabrics & Crafts
joann.com
888-739-4120
fabrics and notions

M & J Trimming
mjtrim.com
212-391-9072
beads and trimmings

Rose Brand
rosebrand.com
800-223-1624

Steinlauf & Stoller
steinlaufandstoller.com
877-869-0321
no-fray and fabric adhesives

Tinsel Trading
tinseltrading.com
212-730-1030
vintage notions

Toho Shoji
212-868-7465
bead store

FAVORS

Apec
apec-usa.com
800-221-9403
glassine envelopes

Atlas Match
atlasmatch.com
800-628-2426
customizable matchbooks

Cyber Island Shops
Seashellworld.com
888-974-3557
all types of shells

Freund Mayer
nostalgicimpressions.com
800-783-0615
wax seals

Glow Sticks
Glowsitckfactory.com
781-773-1120
all sizes

Harvest Import
harvestimport.com
714-368-9188
fabric bags, all sorts

Impact Images
clearbags.com
800-233-2630

JP Trading
jptrading.com
650-871-3940
fans

Matchbooks.com
815-464-2187
matchbooks

Oriental Trading
Orientaltrading.com
1-800-875-8480
seasonal novelties

Pak-Sel
Cellobags.com
503-771-9404
cellophane bags, all sizes

Qualita Paper Products
qualita-paper-products.com
714-540-0994

Sumcards
sumcards.com
212-786-9424
favor bags

Surprise Packages
surprisepackages.com
800-711-3650
boxes and bags

Taylor Corporation
weddingorder.com
favors, stationery, novelties

U.S. Box Corp.
usbox.com
800-221-0999
decorative boxes

US Can
uscanco.com
800-436-6830
tins, all sizes

Vilmain
Vilmain.com
877-243-4494
angel stamped-pewter
medallions

FLORAL SUPPLIES

Bamboo Fencer
bamboofencer.com
617-524-6137

Dry Nature Design
212-695-8911
manzanita branches

Jamali
212-244-4025
bamboo, stones, aisle mats

Lins International
linsinternational.com
800-423-9208
artificial foliage

Oregon Wire Products Co.
oregonwireproducts.com
800-458-8344
wreath frames

Planter Resource
212-206-POTS
containers, glass vases

Save-on-Crafts
831-475-2594
save-on-crafts.com
floral tapes and supplies

PAPER GOODS & PRINTING SERVICES

Century Guild Press
centuryguildpress.com
626-304-0404
letterpress

Continental Corporate Engravers
continentalengravers.com
718-784-7711
engraving, die-cutting, letterpress

DHP Papermill
dhproductions.net
845-228-5926
handmade papers, letterpress

Kate's Paperie
katespaperie.com
888-941-9169
embossers, stationery

Office Depot
888-GO-DEPOT
officedepot.com

Paper Access
800-PAPER-01
PaperAccess.com
papers, tools

Papermart.com
all sorts of bags, papers

Uline.com
800-958-5463
butcher paper, tags, and packaging

Zelda Tannenbaum
718-217-4846
custom-embossed paper

RENTALS

American Rental Association
800-334-2177
to locate rental services in your area

Just Linens
212-688-8808
linens to rent, custom options

Tri Serve Party Rentals
718-822-1930
full-service party rentals

RIBBONS

Brimar
brimarinc.com
800-274-1205

C.M. Offray & Son
212-279-9776
offray.com

Hanah Silk
piecemakers.com
888-321-HANA
hand-died ribbons

Hyman Hendler & Sons
hymanhendler.com
212-840-8393
vintage ribbons

Loose Ends
looseends.com
503-390-7457
raffias, natural

May Arts
mayarts.com
203-637-8366

Midori
midoriribbon.com
800-659-3049

Mokuba
Jkmribbon.com
212-869-8900

TABLETOP

Baccarat
800-777-0100
fine crystal

Crate & Barrel
800-967-6696
crateandbarrel.com
everyday and special occasion

International Silver
syratech.com
617-568-1305
Revere bowls, mint julep cups

Sur la Table
Surlatable.com
800-243-0852
Moroccan glassware

TOOLS

EZ Laminator
EZLaminator.com.
hand-crank laminator

Home Depot
homedepot.com

Save-on-Crafts
831-475-2594
save-on-crafts.com
floral, craft tools

Staples
Staples.com
1-800-333-3330
stationery supplies

Sterling Marking Products
sterling.ca.com
800-265-5957
embossers

Talas
talasonline.com
212-219-0770
book-binding tools, Japanese push drills

credits

Phone numbers or websites appear for providers not included in the resource section on pages 232 to 237.

HALF TITLE PAGE: Rings, Jenny Lessard, 212-481-3788. **TITLE PAGE:** Stemware, Steuben.com. Cocktail, Something Blue by Bacardi. bacardi.com. Crystal appliqué, Swarovski. **COPYRIGHT PAGE:** Charivari chairs, table ware, and linens, Tri Serve Party Rentals.

CHAPTER 1

PAGE 12: Straw runner, Jamali.

PAGE 15: Quilted and lace cloths, Just Linens. Butcher paper, Uline. Garden chairs, Ebay.

PAGE 16: Ribbons, Offray. Paper flowers, Lee Carter Company.

PAGE 19: Glassware, Tri Serve.

PAGE 20: Wreath construction, BlueToadFlowers.com. Candle lamps, Table Decor.

PAGE 23: Chairs, Tri Serve.

PAGE 25: Butcher paper, Uline.

PAGE 26: Chuppah, Blue Meadow Flowers, 212-979-8618. Columns, Ruth Fischl, ruthfischl.com. Stenciled fabric, Angel Threads.

PAGE 29: Floral arbor, Chris Bassett.

PAGE 30: Plastic leaves, Midwest of Cannon Falls. Ribbon, Offray.

PAGE 33: Flowers, Chris Bassett. Chandelier, Casa Allegra. Chandelier crystal, Artifacts.

CHAPTER 2

PAGE 37: Ribbon, Midori. Shells, Dry Nature Design.

PAGE 41: Japanese lanterns, Dry Nature Design.

PAGE 42: Boutonnieres, Two Design Group, tdgevents.com. Pearl pins, jewelry toggles, Jo-ann Fabrics & Crafts.

PAGE 45: Glass beads and beading supplies, abeadstore.com.

PAGE 46: Basket, Jo-ann Fabrics & Crafts. Ribbons, Hannah Silk. Tassel, Brimar.

PAGE 48: Pomander, Stone Kelly Events, 212-875-0500.

PAGE 50: Shell, Dry Nature Design. Feathers, Jo-ann Fabrics & Crafts.

PAGE 53: Vintage handkerchief, Trouvaille Francais, 212-737-6015.

CHAPTER 3

PAGE 57: Ribbons, Offray. Chair, Tri Serve Party Rentals.

PAGE 58: Grommets kit, Jo-ann's Fabrics & Crafts.

PAGE 61: Silk flowers and tassels, TinselTrading.

PAGE 62: Custom sewing, Just Linens.

CHAPTER 4

PAGE 67: Hurricane, Crate & Barrel. Morrocan-style tumblers, Berber Imports.

PAGE 68: Cake pedestal, Abigails.

PAGE 71: Acrylic troughs, Industrial Plastics.

PAGE 72: Birdcage, A Rustic Garden. Feather butterflies, Pany.

PAGE 75: Brass base, Grand Street Lighting. Manzanita branch, Dry Nature.

PAGE 80: Mercury glass compote, Abigails.

PAGE 83: Cloth, chairs, Tri Serve Party Rentals. Pedestal vase, Abigails. Rock sugar, NY Cake & Baking. Goblets, Dorian Webb. Candles, Robb Steck.

PAGE 84: Vase, Abigails. Pearls, Jo-ann's Fabrics & Crafts.

PAGE 87: Square bowls, Crate & Barrrel.

PAGE 88: Copper tray, Smith & Hawken.

CHAPTER 5

PAGE 93: Ice bucket, Midwest of Cannon Falls. Calligraphy, Stephannie Barba. Metal star confetti, Design Ideas. Crystal drops, Save-on-crafts.com.

PAGE 95: Escort cards, CenturyGuildPress.com. Calligraphy, Karin Gable. Ribbon, Midori.

PAGE 97: Garland, R and B Imports.

PAGE 98: Die-cut discs, Continental Corporate Engravers. Calligraphy, Nancy Howell. Wired leaves, Pany.

PAGE 101: Acrylic boxes, Industrial Plastics. Lettering, XYZ Ink. Confetti, SKD Trading.

PAGE 102: Bucket, Schylling. Contact paper, Home Depot.

PAGE 105: Avery crack-and-peel labels, Office Depot.

PAGE 106: Calligraphy, Stephannie Barba. Butcher paper, Uline. Glassware, Crate & Barrel. Dinnerware, Williams-Sonoma.

PAGE 109: Acrylic rings, Industrial Plastics. Lettering, XYZ Ink.

PAGE 113: Acrylic tiles, Industrial Plastics.

PAGE 114: Calligraphy, Anna Pinto. Menu graphics, Kayo DerSarkissian. Glassine envelope, Apec.

CHAPTER 6

PAGE 118: Glass, Julisca. Bamboo skewers, Williams-Sonoma. Beads and paper leaves, Tinsel Trading. Petals, Pany. Metallic tape, Exposures.

PAGE 121: Label artwork, Stephannie Barba.

PAGE 122: Acrylic square, Industrial Plastics. Crystal appliqué, Swarovski. Monogram artwork, Stephannie Barba.